CW01646431

Meanderings in Moyrhee

Growing up in a remote part of County Clare in the 1950's and 1960's

John Brew

ISBN No. 978-1-3999-9546-7

For my wife Connie, my daughter Emily and my son Jonathan

I am so grateful for your support, for your constructive criticism, and for encouraging me to continue writing.

Also, thanks are due to my brother Francis, and my sisters Gerita and Rose for reading the script and not finding too much wrong with it.

Table of Contents

Introduction

We all understand that a river meanders as it makes its way through the surrounding terrain, and the Moyrhee River in County Clare is no exception. It joins the Fergus River near Dromore woods and the Fergus, in turn, flows into the Shannon estuary. Thus, one could say that the water flowing through the mile or so of the Moyrhee river as it passes through the farm where we grew up, winds up contributing to the mighty Atlantic Ocean. I never really thought of it like that when I lived there. The river seems to meander even more around our place than anywhere else, though it may well be the case that that perception is merely a product of my imagination. Like all rivers, it brings life to the area, not just in terms of water supply, but also in terms of the flora and fauna all around it. Before we had running water in our house, we took our water from the river. I should know, having hauled two buckets of water home from the river hundreds of times. It also supplied us with electricity for a time. Many people caught fish in the river, including my two brothers, James and Francis (but not me; more of that later). Francis is also something of a marksman with a shotgun and so the wild duck on the river were at his mercy, as were the pheasants in the woods nearby. Our flock of tame geese spent a good part of the year on the river. We spent time on the river ourselves in the boats that Francis built. And we bathed in shallow parts of it on hot summer days. Yes, it brought life to us, but it could so easily have brought death too. I lost count of the many close shaves I had, almost falling into the same waters. And, of course, none of us were very good swimmers. An ancestor of ours, Tom Brew, did fall in and drown, long ago. The refrain we always heard about him was that "he was swept away in the raging torrent".

Just like any of us, a river can have a changing cast to its countenance every single day. The stretch of the river close to our home featured parts where it was shallow and safe. Other parts were so black and so deep, they appeared to be bottomless. In fine summer weather, the river presented an appearance so peaceful you could barely tell it was flowing at all. But when it was heavily flooded, which happened at least once every year, it covered great swathes of the surrounding ground and took on a much more majestic outlook. Occasional visits from swans brought grace and beauty to the waters. Further on past our home place, the Moyrhee River plays a trick on us, disappearing underground for a stretch, and then reappearing shortly before it joins the Fergus. Perhaps I am deluding myself in thinking that growing up close to such an amenity somehow influences one's personality, and may even be character-forming; in a positive way, one would hope.

I myself also meandered around the general area as I grew up, and this book is an attempt to summarise some of the people and events that I consider to be worth recalling. It is not intended to be a comprehensive account of life on a small farm in the West of Ireland in the 1950's and 1960's. There are many others better equipped than me to do that. Neither is it intended as an autobiography. All I hope for is that readers may find it entertaining.

Early Days

On 26th July 1944, my father, Frank Brew, and my mother, Nancy Quinn, each married a stranger. Arranged marriages were still quite common and theirs was one such. Prior to their wedding day, they had met on only a few carefully-organised occasions, and these were usually supervised. Had they met "by accident", as it were, in the normal way of things, it is unlikely they would ever have formed a long-term relationship, their personalities were so different.

Also, in what would be seen today as bizarre circumstances, it was a "double wedding", in that my mother's brother Andrew was married to Bridgie on the same occasion. The wedding "breakfasts", as they were in those days, were both held in the same place, Glynn's Hotel in Gort, one upstairs and one downstairs.

I know they say opposites attract, and differing personas may complement each other, but, believe me, this would not have been the case when it came to Mam and Dad. To illustrate this, the simplest example I can think of is to outline the manner in which each of them conducted a simple task such as opening a sealed envelope. When the daily post arrived, if my mother happened to be the one on the spot, she would immediately rip open the envelope with her fingers, making tatters of it in the process. That's because she was impulsive, impatient and perhaps just a tad irrational. Dad, by contrast, was usually cool, patient and logical. His approach would be to firstly locate a suitable instrument such as a sharp knife, and then carefully slit an opening along the top of the envelope in such a way that the contents could be easily returned inside it again, if necessary. Despite these contrasts, they eventually learned to live with each other, not without the odd drama along the way, mind you. They successfully reared and saw to the education of six of us, me being the second youngest. We did our best to accept and learn to practice some of their better values such as honesty, fairness and respect. And, of course, we also did our best to ignore what we considered to be their old-fashioned, out-dated and irrelevant belief systems. Much the same as all families then, I suppose.

Dad and Mam on honeymoon in 1944

My earliest memory is not of my Mam or Dad at all, but of my Auntie Bridie. My mother's sister, she had joined an order of nuns at an early age. Along with some other young nuns in the same order, she was then shipped to India. None of them believed that they would ever see home or their families again. But in the early 1950's, things changed and they were allowed to travel home for a short holiday. I was a toddler and apparently liked to nestle in her lap. She gave me my first haircut. When asked "Who cut your hair?" I am told that I would reply on cue, "The nun did". I can just barely recall playing with the large crucifix that hung about her neck, and no more. Officially, in the order to which she belonged, she was "Sister Basil", but to us she would always be Auntie Bridie. Occasional letters would arrive from India. These were always in the special "Air Mail" envelope that was such a common sight in Irish homes then, letters from Irish emigrants all over the world. The Air Mail envelope was an ingenious conception as it did not involve any traditional writing stationery, as such. The writer wrote all over the inside of the envelope itself and then it was folded and addressed in such a manner that it assumed the proportions and appearance of a normal envelope - except, of course, for the fact that it was clearly labelled "Air Mail" and was emblazoned with the unmistakable red and blue livery all around the edge. In an attempt to cram in as much information as possible, the writer would cover every square millimetre of space inside, writing all along the edges, down the sides, everywhere. I wonder if these things still even exist. Auntie Bridie would return to Ireland on several subsequent occasions, most recently in the 1990's when she visited our home in Dublin. This turned out to be her final visit to Ireland before she died in India. I took her to the airport for her departure. She was an extraordinary woman, quite eccentric, and yet also quite charming. I think I could almost write a book about just those few hours I spent in her company at the airport.

Another of my mother's sisters, our Aunt Josie, had also emigrated at a young age; she travelled to San Antonio in Texas, where she made a life for herself and her daughter Mary Jo. They also visited

Ireland for the first time when I was a young boy, in the 1950's. This was at a time when transatlantic travel was still largely conducted by sea, so they travelled by liner to the port of Cobh in Cork. They flew over and back for visits in later years, in the 1960's. Citizens of the United States, or 'Yanks', as they were always incorrectly referred to, were truly exotic creatures to us. I suppose some of it was down to how they dressed, but I think there was much more to it than that – they just appeared more confident, more outgoing than we were. And of course the Texas accent was something else entirely. Even the American cigarettes they smoked looked so much more elegant and glamorous than anything local. I observed that the cigarette packets themselves were quite different too; soft and shiny and not at all anything like the boring cardboard Irish fag-packets. Yes, they brought their own American cigarettes with them, and I believe it was at that time I decided that I was definitely going to be a smoker too, and as soon as I possibly could. They occasionally presented us with one of the most exciting items you could wish for; American dollars, which they could probably ill afford. The generally accepted view, of course, was that practically all Americans were millionaires, and now that there was a Kennedy of Irish descent in the White House, well, that just meant that Irish-Americans could be millionaires as well. Another detail that always impressed me was that when Americans took photographs, something they liked to do quite a lot, the resultant prints always recorded the month and year on the border just beside the actual photograph. In this part of the world we had to wait for digital photography to arrive some decades later before we had the option to feature such metadata.

Another one of my memories from furthest back is waking up on a summer evening, having been put to bed early, as is normally the case with small children. I could hear some of my older siblings running around outside, shouting and playing and generally having a great time. I felt really left out. So, naturally, I went downstairs to join the fun. They had been left to "mind the house", a great rural tradition when adults needed to go somewhere for a while. Part of the responsibility of "minding the house" would be to ensure that the "baby", namely me, would be occasionally checked, and ideally, would still be fast asleep when my parents returned. My older sisters and brothers were horrified to see me up and about. Instead of inviting me to join in the fun and frolics like I expected, they just stood around in a group staring at me, as though I were some type of alien that had burst in and ruined everything. I wanted to say "Come on, keep playing, and let me join in", but I was unable to express that in so many words. I can just recall feeling really frustrated and disappointed. A stand-off ensued until my parents got back and packed me off to bed again.

Like many small children, I had been accustomed to sleeping in a cot. The sides of the cot consisted of a series of vertical metal bars a couple of inches apart from each other. As is usually the case, I was promoted to sleeping in a normal bed, when my parents considered I was age-appropriate for such a transfer. On one of the very first nights in the bed, I unfortunately fell out of it while I was sleeping. Hearing the sound effects from downstairs, my mother called out to know what the matter was. In my confusion I answered 'I fell out through the bars of the cot.'

When I was still at pre-school age, and also still the youngest in the family, I sometimes accompanied my Dad around the place, as he busied himself with various farm-related activities. I have a vague memory of him hauling the remains of an old horse-drawn mowing machine from one of the fields back to the farmyard. I had no idea what he was up to. Over a period of time, he modified the machine, in the process fitting a car dynamo to it. Then he fitted the entire thing in a weir on the river and ran cables to the house, carrying the electricity it generated. We had a PYE radio that had two different types of battery, a common enough arrangement in those times. One of these batteries was rechargeable, and normally required to be taken to town when recharging was needed. The electricity from the river could now be used for this purpose, as well as providing electric light for part of the house. We had green hydro-electricity long before it became a politically correct thing to have.

My only grandparent that was still alive when I was young was my mother's mother, the lady we called 'Granny Quinn'. She sometimes came to stay with us for a while. She seemed a gentle but slightly strange and rather remote figure to us; a little old woman, dressed in black, as so many old women were at that time. She had not had an easy life. Eighteen pregnancies resulted in just nine surviving children. Occasionally, she would take off for a walk through the fields on her own, with the stated intention of collecting sticks for the fire. There was no need for sticks to be collected in this way, as there was always an adequate amount of firewood right outside our back door. I think it was just an excuse for her to wander around on her own. On more than one such occasion, we discovered her lying by a hedge, fast asleep in the summer sunshine. She liked to read and one of her favourite books was our copy of 'Black Beauty'. Like many of her generation, she had grown up in an agrarian society, where the horse was held in very high esteem. This had little to do with a general fondness for large animals; it was to do with survival, for, in the days before large-scale rural mechanisation, a strong and healthy horse was essential to the successful accomplishment of many agricultural activities. She took the 'Black Beauty' story quite seriously, and was aghast at the cruel treatment meted out by the less scrupulous owners of the unfortunate animal. "Oh, that awful man, and the way he treated that lovely horse, it's a pure disgrace", she would declare. It is a slightly peculiar thing to have to admit now, but as far as I can recall, none of us ever really established much of a relationship with the only grandparent that we ever knew.

Another elderly relative was our grand-uncle, also called Frank Brew. He lived just a couple of miles over the road, and sometimes cycled over for a visit on a Sunday afternoon. When we were growing up he was already in his seventies or eighties, and so seemed like an incredibly ancient individual. Also, he sported a moustache, not a common thing at the time, and that made him appear even older. Apparently he was one of the first people in the area to have a bicycle and also, a camera. Deploying the glass plate system, he captured local people in his photographs, none of which survive, to my knowledge. A very quiet and gentle man, he was soft-spoken with a really low voice. He would call us over to him while he sat in the armchair and proceed to tell long, rambling stories, or what I assumed were long, rambling stories, as I could not discern a single word of what he said. It was worth it though, as he always brought us Frys Chocolate Cream bars, one of our favourites. You can still get them. Quite late in life, when he was becoming rather frail, he called over for a special visit. He wanted to take a walk through some of the areas of rough territory nearby, where he had spent his youth, way back in the 1880's and 1890's. He asked me to assist him on his final nostalgic walkabout. I was about thirteen at the time, and like a typical teenager, I found his pace so slow and difficult, I began to fear I would never get him back alive. He sensed my frustration, but rather than become irritated with me, which he would have had every right to do, he simply said; "Old bones are brittle, Johnny, old bones are brittle."

I can just about recall the first time I attended a funeral. I did not know who had died, but it must have been some local man, since the burial took place in a cemetery just about a mile from our home. I think my mother simply took me along with her for company. I had a very rough idea what to expect, but nevertheless, the first time a small child witnesses a coffin being lowered into the ground and covered up with earth, it is certainly an unforgettable experience. Following lengthy prayers from the priest, the two grave-diggers placed their shovels on top of the piled earth in the form of a cross. Finally, it was the widow's time to take centre stage. Suitably attired in black from head to foot, she threw herself to her knees beside the grave and proceeded to wail, moan and cry in a way that shook me even more than all the preceding scary acts of the ceremony. It was apparent that her late husband's name was Pat, for occasionally she looked up to heaven and cried out loudly, "Oh, why did you have to leave me, Pat?" I have attended many funerals since then, but few that remain so vivid in the memory.

As a matter of interest, in country places such as where we grew up, the gravediggers were always local people. They would usually be neighbours of the deceased person, typically strong young men. Since it is a function which requires a degree of mental as well as physical strength, I believe that it is customary for the bereaved family to supply a bottle of whiskey to the chosen ones, in case they need something to revive their flagging spirits whilst the work is in hand. If you are the type of person that is likely to be upset at the sight of human bones being taken from the ground, then you would not be a suitable candidate for this sort of work. Whenever I have mentioned all this to anyone who grew up in an urban environment, where grave-digging is actually a paid job as such, they find it hard to believe me. I know that my own brother Francis has been called upon on occasions when neighbours passed away.

When my mother finally passed away in December 2023, at the age of 101, the gravediggers were, as always, local men, six of them altogether. But they were not young men, as had traditionally been the case. They were fellows that I had grown up with, one of whom was actually older than me, and I am now in my seventies. I spoke to them after the burial and they explained to me that younger men no longer have the time or the inclination to participate in activities of this nature. What will happen when our generation are all gone?

A 'family' plot or grave is a fairly common thing in many societies and things were no different in the west of Ireland. I remember the day when a man whom I did not know, came to our home and engaged in a long and rather earnest-looking conversation with our Dad. It emerged that he had just attended a funeral, in the course of which he observed that the coffin had been buried in the 'wrong' place, namely it was buried in our family plot. I would have thought that the thing to do would be to say nothing and do nothing; after all, what difference does a thing like that make in the final analysis? But, no, that is not how such matters were viewed. A difficult and complex process had to be initiated, culminating with the coffin being dug up and re-interred in the 'right' place. I was never informed of the identity of the guest that had taken up temporary residence in our plot.

The delivery of a telegram to one's home was almost a certain indication of bad news, the worst possible outcome being that a close relative had died. Very few people in country places had a telephone and so the fastest way to alert all relatives and friends that a death had occurred was by telegram. The arrival of the small green envelope was viewed with great anxiety, until one of our parents actually opened it and announced the name of the departed one. More often than not, this was followed by the relieved statement, 'Oh, thank God, it's only so-and-so'.

Telegrams came through the local Post Office, but they were not usually delivered by the postman. They might be, if he happened to be in the Post Office when the telegram was rung in, but otherwise it was the responsibility of the Post Office staff to see to the delivery of every telegram. And this was a grey area, since they had no staff to carry out this particular function. In cities and large towns, there apparently existed an entity known as a 'telegraph boy', who was paid to deliver telegrams. But in the heart of the country, telegrams were something of a rarity, and telegraph boys were rarer still, that is to say, they did not exist. Sending a telegram was essentially reserved for somewhat urgent matters, and so the intention was that delivery would be completed as quickly as possible, almost like an email or text message today. Ok, not that fast, but pretty fast all the same. Clearly that could not happen in a place like Tubber. What really happened was that the Post Office staff would hand the telegram to an individual who lived not too far away from the addressee and who happened to call into the Post Office during the day. And somebody nearly always would. I once fell victim to this rather hit-and-miss system myself when I was on leave between ships in my job as a Radio Officer in the Merchant Navy in the 1970's. We had no telephone in the house, and so when my employer needed to contact me, it could only be done by telegram. Such a telegram arrived to the Post Office one day and there was no one to deliver it. So, it remained undelivered for the day. That evening I happened to be attending a social event in the parish hall. A lady from the Post Office also attended the event and handed me my telegram. I don't know when I would have received it otherwise. No wonder my Dad wanted to get a telephone.

After decades of postal deliveries by automobile, it has now become a common sight in recent years to witness a postman (or postwoman, I suppose, though I have never seen one of them) going around on a bicycle. But this is just completing a circle. In the 1960's, and before that, all post was delivered by a postman on a bicycle. Our local postman, Eugene O'Loughlin, had to cycle some miles all the way over the long road to where we lived, the very last house on that particular route, even if he only had that one letter for the entire road. And, of course, he covered many other roads in the postal district served by Tubber Post Office. I have been attempting to imagine how many miles he, and, indeed, many other postmen, must have travelled each weekday. Perhaps as much as fifty miles a day or even more, I don't really know. Also, Eugene O'Loughlin was not a local man, and so he firstly had to travel some distance on his bike each day, just to get to his place of work, Tubber Post Office. In a typically ironic twist, the very next house over the road from the Post Office was occupied by another postman, but, needless to say, he was employed in some other postal area. This man was adorned with a slightly larger than usual pair of ears, so, of course, he was commonly known as 'Luggy' – not to his face, though. I wonder if he even knew.

With improving economic conditions in the 1960's, many Irish people who had never previously been in a position to purchase a motor car were now able to do so, and our postman, Eugene, was one of these. But he did not use the car on his postal route. I don't really know the background to this, but I have to assume that postal deliveries by car were simply not approved, or perhaps it was that their expenses would not be covered. So, the ironic thing was that you would see his car abandoned close by the Post Office every weekday as he carried out his deliveries, regardless of weather conditions, on his bicycle. Or, rather, I should say, on his Department of Post and Telegraphs-supplied official bicycle. Not that it struck anyone as ironic at the time. That was just the way it was. In fact, when postal deliveries in rural areas by car started to become the norm in later years, many people considered this to be a crazy and ill-fated departure from tradition. "It's ridiculous", they said. "Sure won't he be getting in and out of the car every couple of minutes?"

"Mixed farming", that's what they called the type of farming that existed on small farms in the West of Ireland, meaning farmers did not concentrate on one particular type of agricultural activity, as they very much did in later decades, concentrating on maybe, milk production or cereal crops or whatever. Back in the fifties and sixties, there was a bit of everything on most farms. Cattle, sheep, oats, wheat, barley, potatoes, sugar beet, mangolds, turnips, the list went on and on. We were lucky also in that we had a richness of fruit to choose from in the summer and autumn months, such as blackcurrants, gooseberries, loganberries and strawberries, as well as an entire orchard full of apples. Possibly my favourite was plums. These grew in a row of trees all the way along the side of one of the fields. The plum-trees were big and strong enough that you could climb up on to them, and I often did so, spending an entire evening munching away on them. I have never since found plums that taste even half as good as they did. Also, working in the tillage-fields, there was no need to go hungry whilst waiting for dinner. In a field with a cereal crop, you could take some and rub it in the palm of your hand, then blow away the husk and eat the remaining grains. You could rip off a cabbage-leaf any time and chew on it. The same applies to lettuce and onions. If you have a knife on you, it is easy to pull up a carrot and clean it for immediate consumption. I suppose if you were really desperate, you could do the same thing with a turnip, although I have to say that I do not recall ever being as hungry as that in the fields; it would be preferable to walk all the way back to the house and get something else. As for wild fruits, well, there are haws and sloes, of course, but, in my opinion, neither of these is fit for human consumption. In the autumn, blackberries were available in vast numbers on hedges everywhere, and were sweet and juicy to taste. You did need to inspect each one carefully, though, as you would occasionally encounter tiny white maggots crawling on them. Wild strawberries are really good, and we did pick them, but you need a lot of them just for a decent mouthful. To carry them along without getting them crushed or damaged, we carefully slid each berry on to a long piece of strong grass. You might end up with five or six such lengths of grass. What you soon learned was that the places where wild strawberries grew were also infested with ticks – tiny insects that somehow attached themselves to your legs. Slowly but steadily crawling up along you they would make for the warmest part of the body, where, naturally, they are least welcome. There, they would sink their blood-sucking mouths into your body, literally feasting on your blood. When you got back to the house it was always a good idea to do a quick body-check, because if you did not, they would then grow as they engorged themselves, becoming disgustingly larger and fatter. Even when you discovered them and got rid of them, they left a strong itchiness behind as a reminder of your own carelessness. When we were little, our Mam would deal with them. Having removed each tick from your skin, she would dispose of it by tossing it on top of the range, where the heat would cause it to quickly expand and then explode with an audible 'pop'. If you have never had your blood sucked by ticks, well, lucky you. If you care to be horrified, then go ahead and do a Google Images search for 'ticks on humans'. The positive aspect of bringing home a good harvest of wild strawberries was the reward to be had from grinding them up with the back of a spoon in a cup, adding some cream and a little sugar. I guarantee you will never taste a better dessert. Wild mushrooms were also an occasional delicacy. These grow best in fields where the grass is cropped down to a very low level, such as where sheep are kept. We never had sheep, so mushrooms were rare in our place. But, luckily, our neighbours, the Connells, did keep sheep, and we knew exactly where to look for the mushrooms each day – they grow overnight, so you can go back to the same place day after day. Back then, neighbours paid little attention to children 'trespassing' on their ground. The recipe for a mini-feast of wild mushrooms was simplicity itself. Place each individual inverted mushroom directly on to the top of the range, which was almost always really hot. Drop in a small piece of butter and an unhealthy dose of salt. Wait a minute or two while it cooks, remove it, blow on it to cool it sufficiently, and then consume it on the spot, standing right there by the range – satisfaction guaranteed.

As well as all the interesting things that you could pick wild and consume, there were, of course, also some that we were warned never to consume, being poisonous. Along the roadside close to our home, in the summertime there grew some vividly-coloured red and yellow berries that looked really attractive. I don't know what they were, but it had been made abundantly clear to us that we were never to even touch them, never mind eat them. One day, the temptation simply became too much. My sister Rose and I sampled one each. They were really quite disappointing, with a very bitter flavour; not at all what we had anticipated. But the really worrying part was that we now feared we had poisoned ourselves, with a strong likelihood that we would quickly succumb to a painful death. The fear of our imminent demise was overshadowed by the fear of our mother's wrath, if we were to confess our immense foolishness to her. Minutes passed, and no symptoms materialised. Then hours passed, and, again, nothing seemed to be happening. But, who knew, perhaps this was a slow-acting poison. It might take a week or a month and in the meantime there was nothing one could do, other than live with the anxiety. Nothing ever became of it, of course, but, then again, perhaps it takes sixty years or so. We may not yet be safe.

The fields on our farm all had names; I believe this was common practice throughout the country back then. Some were named in English, with very simple names such as 'The High Field', 'The Four-

Acre', 'The Small Field', 'The Big Paddock' and 'Ford's Field'. The other fields were named through Irish; interesting-sounding names that I never knew how to spell, nor, indeed, did I even know what they meant. I should have asked my Dad, I know. Even some of the rough areas covered in rocks and bushes were also named in Irish.

We always had cows, and they were rather docile animals. They all looked quite different from each other and thus could be easily identified individually. Each one had a name, but the names were not of the traditional cheesy variety. No, they were named in a way that was simply based on their physical appearance; amongst them I remember 'Blacknose', 'Tall Red', 'Small Red', 'The Grey Cow' and – inevitably, I suppose, - 'Big Tits'. I believe it was my mother who named them. We did not keep sheep, and in any case, I always regarded sheep as somewhat boring animals. After all, they all looked exactly alike. What was the point in cloning Dolly the sheep, when every sheep already looks exactly like Dolly anyway? Dog cloning would have been so much more interesting – we could still have our pet, Lassie. Farmers had to have their flock of sheep branded, otherwise if they strayed from farm to farm and became intermingled, how could anyone tell which sheep were theirs? Then again, what would it matter? Whenever we wandered through neighbours' fields, we were careful to avoid sheep because we were aware that each flock would usually include a ram, and rams were reputed to be angry, aggressive beasts. Mam's advice was that if you were unfortunate enough to be chased by a ram, then rather than running for it, the thing to do was to simply lie prone on the ground, the thinking being that for some reason related to the physical configuration of a ram it was not capable of lowering its head down to the level required for terrorising a low-lying human. I didn't believe her; I determined that in such circumstances I would definitely run like mad, as sheep did not look like very fast movers to me. The theory was put to the test one morning as we walked to school. Somehow, our neighbours' flock of sheep had escaped from their customary field and were out on the road. We carefully squeezed by, but just as we thought we were safe, one of them peeled away from the flock and began to chase us. It was the ram, surely! And, quite worryingly, it was clear that he could move a lot faster than I had ever believed a short-legged, woolly dumb creature could. We had a bit of a head start though and, rounding a corner, we pulled a fast one. We very quickly climbed over a wall into a nearby field and watched as the scary animal stupidly raced past. Now the question was how should we proceed, seeing that the ram was between us and our destination? I had forgotten exactly what we did next, but my sister Gerita recalls that we got to school, field by field, climbing over walls and through fences as we went.

Whatever about sheep, the one animal I really feared the most was the pig. They are dirty, smelly and untrustworthy creatures. People will try to convince you that a pig is an intelligent being. They have been known to eat their young, or even, just roll over on them, crushing them to death – not a great indicator of intelligence there, I'm afraid. The main reason that a farmer would keep at least one pig was to provide bacon. So, about once a year, a man would arrive to perform this function, that is, to kill the pig. When I was a very small boy, the man in question was Mike O'Fitzgibbon. I may have spelled his name wrongly; all I know is that it was pronounced as if it were Miko Fitzgibbon. The entire procedure was extremely frightening to me, everything from the screams of the unfortunate victim as it was dragged to its place of doom, on to its barbaric despatch with a blow to the head from a sledgehammer, followed by the drawing of its blood from having its throat cut, and then chopping the entire animal up into smaller pieces to be salted away in a barrel. The entire spectacle was blood-curdling from start to finish. I was not obliged to watch, of course, and, indeed, I would not have dreamt of leaving the safety of the kitchen whilst the horror was in progress. At the same time, I somehow could not stop myself from climbing on a chair and half-watching it, barely lifting the corner of the net curtain on the window for a slightly better view of something I really did not want to see. Once, when Mr. Fitzgibbon was part way through his gory labours, he came to the kitchen door and spoke to my mother. Perhaps he wanted a drink of water or something, I do not remember. They engaged in some light conversation, which I found to be entirely inappropriate, considering the revolting nature of the circumstances. Then he spotted me, keeping a low profile in the corner of the kitchen. I heard him say to my mother, "Oh, that's a lovely little boy you have there, Mrs. Brew. I suppose I can take him home with me?" He stood there, literally dripping with the blood of the animal he had just so cruelly laid low. Imagine going anywhere with him! Then, to my utmost horror, I heard my mother reply, "Oh, you can of course, Miko. Sure, I have no need for him at all. Take him away there now for yourself". What was she thinking? I would sooner have left the house in the company of Satan himself. I was glad when the day was over, and Mike O'Fitzgibbon departed without me, not to be seen again for another year.

Another custom associated with the ritual slaying of the pig was the practice of delivering some of the fresh meat to various neighbours/friends/relatives. This practice was expected, to the point of almost being regarded as close to compulsory. Not to share the spoils would have been seen as taking a not very community-minded attitude, and, in fairness, there was a rural community of sorts, which, I believe, no longer exists in such places today. Typically, we youngsters were given the responsibility of seeing to these deliveries. This was a job I did not mind, as it could often yield a financial payoff from the beneficiary, as an expression of their gratitude. My younger sister Rose was once entrusted with such a mission. However, the destination she was directed to was not a particular favourite of hers, as she was in some fear of the rather intimidating lady of the house in question. So, having walked some distance, and following a decent interval, she simply returned home, and informed everybody that she had found there was nobody at the house, and so had no choice but to bring the delivery back home again. Our parents were very surprised, as the home in question was well known to be almost always fully populated, not just with its own family members, but also with passing neighbours, many of whom would drop in for a visit practically every single day.

On another day whilst on a visit to the house in question, the scary lady served Rose with a salad that included a whole tomato on the plate. In a futile attempt to slice the tomato, not only did the offending fruit squelch out from under the knife and escape from Rose's grasp, but she also succeeded in quite badly cutting her finger, which began to pump blood. The last thing she needed was for the scary lady to see her predicament and make a big deal about it, so Rose concealed her injury by wrapping the damaged digit in the folds of her light blue dress, which was, of course, ruined by the copious nature of the bleeding. Rose also recalls one occasion when the admittedly well-intentioned woman presented her with a going-home gift of two half-crowns; not an insignificant sum for a child at that time. Unfortunately, Rose lost the two valuable coins on the walk home.

I was also a bit wary of the scary woman. She was not a bad person or anything, quite the contrary in fact; she was actually generous to a fault. It was her manner that was an issue for us. I did not have the courage or the brains to do what Rose had done with the pigmeat, so when I was sent to that house, I always completed my mission. At home we were accustomed to drinking our tea from mugs, whilst sitting at a plain wooden table. But the lady of this house would insist that you have your tea at a fancy table with a tablecloth, and complete with a dainty cup and saucer – the whole shebang. The atmosphere made me nervous, and more likely to spill stuff. If you did not let her know that you had finished your first cup of tea, she would verbally dress you down for not quickly alerting her to the fact that a second fill of the cup was called for – whether you wanted it or not. She might even deliver a little slap for not allowing her to adequately fulfil her function of making sure that everyone was absolutely topped up with tea and cake at all times. I would try to make the cup of tea last as long as possible, so that there could be no justification for a second; but it was no use, she was on to that subterfuge too. She would now complain that you had let your tea go cold, and had not drawn her attention to the need for a warming top-up. Really, one was up against it, and simply could not win.

Perhaps I am giving the impression that, as a small child, I was something of a 'wimp' or a 'scaredy-cat'. Well, fair enough, I suppose, that is what I was. For instance, one of the highlights of the summer season every year would be a trip to the seaside at Lahinch. After we had passed through the small town of Ennistymon, we would very shortly thereafter come into view of the ocean itself, then just a couple of miles away. My siblings were all around me in the back of the car, at this point beside themselves with excitement. But the sight of the sea on the horizon always frightened the living daylights out of me. It seemed to have the terrifying appearance of a 'wall of water' or indeed what we would now identify as a 'tsunami'. Of course, I could not expose my fear to the rest of the family; that would imply weakness, never a good sign. And, anyway, within minutes we were there, and I immediately forgot all about my terrible conviction that we would all be washed away – until the next time. How did I ever end up going to sea before I was even twenty?

We did not necessarily always need to drive to the seaside, as there was a small narrow-gauge railway that from ran from Ennis to Lahinch and various other places, until it was torn up and done away with in the early 1960's. Apparently the tracks were sent to some developing country in Africa. The 'West Clare Railway' was made famous in a Percy French song of the time. We could get on board at a station somewhere near Corofin for the onward journey to Lahinch. Perhaps I travelled on the line more than once, I really don't know, but I do recall making the journey on at least one occasion. I must have been very young as I can now recall only two things about it. One is that, unlike a 'normal' train, the seats were longitudinally arranged by the windows, facing each other, much like the 'Tube' in London. The second memory I have is of the train arriving into Ennistymon, one of the last stops on the way to Lahinch. At every stop, a group of young boys had not been able to resist showing off their ability to read the sign on the platform, by calling out the name of each station as the train pulled in. And so now they shouted; 'Innishtymon! Innishtymon!' The vernacular demanded that an extra letter 'h' was appended to the letter 's'. My mother was not impressed. 'Don't mind those boys', she said to me. 'It's not Innishtymon, it's Ennistymon.' I never forgot.

Travel by train is now an unheard of luxury in the kind of remote place where we lived, and has been since the 1960's when all the rural railway stations were shut down. I remember travelling to the local town of Ennis by train from the tiny station near our local village in Tubber. The train stopped in various other similar stations along the way, so, naturally, took quite a while to get to town. Nevertheless, it did always get there – that is, until the powers-that-be deemed that it was no longer economically viable. The prevailing wisdom was that people were becoming better off and so almost every family could afford a car; the train was seen as belonging to the past. Now, the prevailing wisdom seems to be that we should get out of our cars and get on board the train. But in the case of the small rural type of railway station that had served the surrounding community so well for so long, well, I'm afraid that that train has indeed well and truly pulled out of the station, having finally done so well over half a century ago. Taking the train from Galway to Ennis a few years ago, I found it difficult to even spot these very small old station-houses as we flashed by.

From the mid 1940's, CIE was the Irish national public transport company, running trains and buses over much of the country. The CIE logo was, appropriately enough, I suppose, a "flying wheel". It was a classic design, but in the mid-sixties, in a misguided effort to modernise that went disastrously wrong, the logo was changed for, incredibly, a "broken wheel". Sadly, it turned out to be somewhat prophetic, as the company endured many "broken" years of strikes, closedowns of railway lines and massive financial losses. Apparently, CIE, as an entity, still exists, but the embarrassing logo is carefully hidden. It used to adorn every bus, every train engine and carriage, as well as the fleet of trucks that delivered kegs of Guinness to pubs all over the country.

My parents' trips to the local town of Ennis were common enough, I suppose every few weeks or so. Mam and Dad would always bring back something of interest to us youngsters, such as sweets or, best of all, comics like the Beano or the Dandy. We were all serious comic aficionados. On one occasion, when I was almost four years old, they brought back something totally new, different and unexpected. My mother had been away for a few days; I had no idea where she was, just being told that she would be back soon. And, indeed, she did come back. I noticed Dad rushing into the house, carrying something small, which he took directly upstairs. Nobody told me a thing about what was going on, but in time, I discovered that I was no longer "the baby". There was a new one, a real baby, my sister Rose.

I often felt that I was somehow "out of the loop" as described above. Things would happen, I might or might not be aware of them, but the truth would usually dawn on me – eventually. Now, with the great benefit of hindsight, I see the reality, and it's very simple; I was right all the time, I was left out of the loop. Not through any deliberate intent on anyone's part, I think it was just too much trouble to be explaining everything to a pesky little kid. The standard reply to this is "But, you should have been asking questions". If you had older sisters or brothers, you would know that asking them questions is mostly a useless exercise. My experience was that the standard reply from older siblings would be along the lines of, "You eejit, you mean you don't even know that?" There was no malice intended, it was just the way these things were handled. A good example is the whole business of learning to read the time on a standard old-fashioned analogue clock face. There were no digital clocks, or talking clocks, you just had to learn to read the time, and it was a very hard thing to do. Everyone else could tell the time, and for ages, maybe for years, I hid the fact that I could not. You would be surprised what you can get away with and the ingenious ways you learn to avoid the potential humiliation of having your dirty secret exposed. Once, my brother Francis and a local friend of his called Micky Grady were out exploring the rough terrain across the far side of the Moyrhee river. For once, they brought me along with them. Micky had to be home by a certain time, and not having a timepiece (nobody had), he asked me to run back to the house and find out the time. I ran, while furiously thinking of what I was going to do. Under pressure, I came up with a cunning plan, though I doubted it could work. When I got to the house, I stopped at the kitchen window, feigning exhaustion, and relying on the knowledge that there was always likely to be at least one person in there, I called out; "Micky Grady wants to know the time". Magically, it worked. Somebody told me the time. I memorized it, though the words meant very little, ran back to the lads and triumphantly reported the time of day. Disappointingly, Micky didn't seem all that interested, after all. Even so, I was elated. My secret was still safe.

That same neighbouring fellow, Micky Grady, was very handy with mechanical things in his teenage years. I believe he became a fitter later in life. He actually constructed his own home-made shotgun, assembled from various pieces of metal he collected from wherever he could. Farmyards were full of scrap metal. I believe the barrel was originally part of a bicycle frame. It was somewhat crude, with much of the working parts visible to the naked eye. I think he deployed a steel nail for the firing pin. Nevertheless, it apparently worked, though I personally never saw it in action. Micky knew that his Dad would never allow a dangerous object of that nature to exist anywhere about their own farm, so he kept it in our place instead, my parents apparently taking a more liberal view of such matters. So, for quite a while, perhaps a year or more, we kept an illegal, unlicensed, potentially lethal firearm at our premises. Thinking about my parents' easy-going attitude reminds me that Dad once made me a crossbow. OK, it was relatively harmless as weapons of this nature go, and it was wildly inaccurate, nevertheless it was a genuine crossbow, and if used in the wrong way, it could have wreaked havoc, I am sure.

I do not remember when or how I learned to read the time, but somehow I eventually managed it. When you think about it, the system of time measurement and the methods of displaying it are ridiculously and unnecessarily complex. For example, what genius came up with the concept of sixty seconds in a minute? Why sixty? One hundred would have been so much better. The same goes for the number of minutes in an hour. And as for twenty-four hours, broken down into two sets of twelve, well that was just pure genius, I suppose. There is an alternative and vastly superior method, and it was introduced in France around the time of the Revolution. Unfortunately, they ultimately reverted to the sub-optimal system we are stuck with to this day. The concept is simple; one hundred seconds in a minute, one hundred minutes in an hour, and ten hours in a full day. Thus, five o'clock would be midday, for example. The total number of seconds in a day is not that different; 86,400 for the current, almost unworkable system, compared to 100,000 for the superior method. Since there would be about 15% more seconds in the day, then, of course, each second would be slightly shorter than what we are accustomed to – no big deal. Apparently, you can still view some of these clocks in Paris. Perhaps I will live to see the day when it becomes the standard system of time measurement; I'm not very hopeful about that though.

Explaining the functions of the hands on a typical clock face to a child for the first time has to be a most challenging experience. There are three hands to be accounted for. As some comedian once pointed out, the first hand is the hour hand, the second hand is the minute hand, and (most incredibly and most difficult to justify) the third hand is the second hand. Yes, "the third hand is the second hand!" Could it have been made any more difficult? I don't know now how I ever came to grips with it. I don't know how anyone comes to grips with it.

Despite my late arrival to the world of timepieces and how to use them, the entire business of clocks and time measurement has featured to a surprising degree in my career. As a Marine Radio Officer in the merchant navy, part of my daily duties was to ensure the accuracy of time measurement on board ship through the use of radio time signals and on-board chronometers. This was essential for accurate navigational measurements – until the arrival of GPS systems, which can yield very accurate display of time of day as well as exact location. Subsequently, I worked for some years in software development, mainly engaged in, yes, you might have guessed it, real-time systems. Later, working as a Broadcast Engineer in radio, I found myself with responsibility for, amongst many other things, maintaining and renewing the in-house system for driving studio clocks and for providing accurate time for the in-house computer network.

Getting Older

The best way to get around was on a bicycle, and we all learned to cycle by riding around the fields, before taking the risk of venturing on to the public road. We were not even aware of the existence of such a thing as a child-sized bicycle, and so, from the age of about five or six, we trained on adult bikes that were way too big for us. In those days a 'woman's' bicycle did not have a bar between the saddle and the handlebars so that was a bit easier to manage. But using a 'man's' bicycle meant sticking one leg underneath the bar to reach the pedal on the other side. This necessitated a rather delicate balancing act, with the entire bike at a peculiar angle to the ground - very demanding for a young child, especially one that was a novice to the art of cycling, and on the uneven surface of an agricultural field. You soon learned to fall in a way that minimised injury. We had never even heard of such a thing as a cycling helmet. Once you had mastered the basics of cycling, however, you could then ride a bike just about anywhere. We never had any means of securing or locking up our bikes. Such measures were unnecessary, bicycle theft being a very rare thing, and when and if it did happen, it was viewed in a similar manner to the heinous crime of stealing a cowpoke's horse in the days of the Wild West. Years later, when the time eventually came for learning to drive a car, we used the exact same training ground, namely the fields closest to the house.

I remember being brought to the doctor more than once when I was a small boy, not because I was sick or anything, but purely because I was thin. Well, a bit too thin, I suppose. It is more common now for children to require medical attention for the opposite reason i.e. for obesity. There were almost no obese kids to be seen in our part of the world in the fifties and sixties. The doctor in question, Doctor Marlborough, had his surgery in his large and rather imposing red-brick house in the middle of the main street in the town of Gort. The one really positive thing that I recall from his room was the swivel chair in which we were allowed to spin round and round. There was no such thing to be seen anywhere else locally that I can recall. I don't believe Doctor Marlborough stumbled on a miracle cure for my affliction; I was a very thin person right up until my early twenties. Of course, I have made up for it since then, gradually becoming less and less thin, as the years went by. But when I was still a boy, I was the yardstick by which thinness was gauged. If my mother ran into an acquaintance that appeared to have lost a great deal of weight, for example, she might say, 'That poor woman doesn't look well at all. She is as thin as Johnny.'

Parents were convinced, of course, that cod liver oil was the cure for just about anything, and that included being too thin, so from time to time we were dosed with the stuff. It was absolutely vile and ghastly to taste, and, as far as anybody can tell, it yielded no benefit whatsoever. Also, parents appear to have been indoctrinated into believing that children could develop worms in their internal system. How exactly this was meant to come about, I cannot even begin to imagine, but it does sound very scary, one must admit. Needless to say, doctors and pharmacists had the remedy for this as well, or perhaps not so much a remedy as a preventative measure. It was a type of powder which came wrapped up in a little piece of paper. To the naked eye it appeared quite innocuous, but the reality was a different matter. I learned to greatly fear the experience. Our mother added water to the powder and tried to persuade us to drink the resulting concoction. I have never in my life since tasted anything quite so frightful. The dreadful flavour made cod liver oil seem like strawberries and cream by comparison. Mam tried to help me to overcome the extremely repulsive nature of the experience by feeding me a spoonful of sugar immediately following the dosage. It was entirely unintentional on her part, but the mental association of poisonous-tasting medicine with sugar had the unanticipated consequence of making me unable to consume sugar for quite a long time afterwards – perhaps not a bad thing in itself. On one such occasion, oranges had been brought from town. Normally this would be quite a treat. But having the taste of an orange immediately after the medicine had the same result, namely that for many years I could not stomach oranges without recalling the foul nature of that powdery stuff. In general, our childhoods were happy times, but if I had to pick the lowest of low points, I think that would be it.

On the other hand, if I were asked to recall a particularly happy occasion, strangely enough it would not necessarily be a birthday or a Christmas morning. Instead, it was a fine summer morning as we walked over the road to do some work in the fields. I was still quite small so I was not there to be productive – I just followed along with the others. I cannot recall exactly which other members of the family were present, apart from Dad, who was leading a horse. As we walked along, the sun shone through the trees that arched over the road, giving a dappled effect. I still love dappled sunlight on a summer's day. I was old enough to participate and yet young enough not to have any real responsibility. I realise that it sounds like a very ordinary occasion, and indeed that is exactly what it was, but, for whatever reason, I have never forgotten it. Everything was just fine.

In my youth, children's birthdays were not the elaborate affairs they are today. Nevertheless, my parents usually organised something for the day, even if it was just a sponge cake. That was good enough. For my eighth birthday, I suspected they had completely forgotten, as there did not appear to be anything special on the agenda. Our dog, Blackie, had recently had pups and just one of them was kept. We called her Lassie. You can tell how great we were with dogs' names. I believe someone had the ingenious idea that I could be told Lassie was my birthday present. I was delighted of course. Not long after that, Lassie's mother Blackie chased a truck and paid the ultimate price for doing so. Lassie became the farm dog, regardless of whether she was really mine or not. I think everybody else conveniently forgot, but secretly, I always regarded Lassie as my dog. She was a working dog and our pet for a long time, even for some years after I had left home and gone away to sea.

Lassie and me

Very few people today would know what a 'gramophone' was, or certainly very few would ever have seen one, never mind heard one. It was the record player or turntable of its day, used to play the old, large and heavy discs that rotated at 78 rpm. These had been around since the early part of the twentieth century, and were still manufactured right into the mid-fifties. Apparently some of Elvis's earliest recordings were released in the '78' format. Before radio sets had become commonplace household items, the only artificial form of entertainment in many homes was a gramophone, and some of them were still around when we were young. It did not require an electrical supply or any form of external connection, being powered by the simple act of winding a handle on the side. This kept the thing going just long enough to play one record. There was a gramophone in our parlour and a stack of 78-style discs. I do not recall our parents ever using it, but in times of extreme boredom, we sometimes did. The big problem was that all the recordings consisted of material that was quite boring to us, stuff such as arias from operas and songs performed by John McCormack.

The turntable had a variable speed control, so you could have some fun with that, slowing the performance down so that it sounded like some kind of death-knell, or, better still, speeding it up, so that it sounded like chipmunks. My older sister Gerita and I came up with an ingenious method of extracting much more entertainment from the gramophone. As with all record players, a little dexterity needed to be deployed in placing the stylus, which was basically a rough needle, on to the spinning disc. Our younger sister Rose was little more than a toddler at the time and we used to persuade her that this feat was well within her grasp. It was not. We would wind up the gramophone, hand her a disc, and let her get on with it. Meanwhile, we quickly left the room, usually climbing halfway up the stairs that was just outside the parlour door. We sat on the stairs, and, presently, you would hear the dreadful scraping and scratching sounds of the needle being dropped repeatedly all over the record. You might even hear some snatches of music. Many of the house collection of 78's were absolutely ruined in this manner. The discs were somewhat fragile, so, as well as getting badly scratched, they would shatter if dropped. Of course, Gerita and I were not even in the room when the damage was done, so, in all fairness, we could not be held responsible, now, could we?

There were various other ways to amuse ourselves, especially on wet days when we were stuck in the house. One of the rooms had large stacks of documents that were left over from the time Dad had been in the LDF, or Local Defence Force. At first, we thought it was fun to pretend we were soldiers and fill our names in over and over again. That kind of thing is alright for a while, but we soon found it was more fun to just throw reams of the stuff out the window. When I was the youngest, my older siblings encouraged me to be the destructive vandal, so that they would not be blamed, just as Gerita and I did later to Rose with the gramophone records. Most of the stuff we dumped was just blank forms, but I'm pretty sure there were filled-in forms amongst them as well, documents that would certainly be of historical interest today. Well, too bad, they are almost all gone.

Now that I look back on these activities, what I find most interesting is that I do not recall that there were ever any repercussions forthcoming from Mam or Dad, not even as much as a mild verbal rebuke. I don't know if it was that they didn't care, or they never found out, or maybe they were just very tolerant, easy-going parents; I suspect it was the latter. For instance, I was in the habit of kicking a football against the wall of the house. Sometimes, my aim was not so good, and I might hit the kitchen window, with the inevitable result. Dad was handy at everything, and that included cutting glass to shape, fitting putty and so on. I do not recall him ever telling me to take the football out to the field where it belonged.

Thinking of football reminds me that, as a young lad, I once won a Gaelic football in a competition. There was a children's column in the Saturday edition of The Irish Press daily newspaper called Captain Mac's Club. I was a member. For many years I even had the little shiny metal badge to prove it. I wonder what became of that badge. Captain Mac's club held weekly competitions, and I soon found that if you entered regularly, you would actually win the occasional prize. I remember winning a torch, and, of course, the football. It was a genuine leather GAA football. In those days a GAA-approved football was a formidable object. It had an inner type of tube or bladder, which you inflated, and then the outer leather section actually had to be laced up. Of course, I was immensely proud of it. But, there was a problem. Because it was real leather, it soaked up water. Fields in the west of Ireland seem to contain more water than anything else. The ball would quickly become so waterlogged it was like trying to kick a stone around the field. Dad, who knew everything, recommended stuff called 'Dubbin', which apparently was used to protect leather. He even got it for me. It only worked up to a point, soon wearing off. Because I had won the ball, and because I was so proud of it, I persisted with it for years, when I should have just kicked the damn thing into the river, and got an ordinary plastic ball. But I just could not let it go. From time to time in life, I have found myself hoarding things that would be better let go, just like that football.

There was also a children's crossword in the Sunday Press, which we regularly entered and won. If I remember rightly, the monetary prizes were actually in guineas! My mother, who considered herself a good judge of women's clothes, always entered the 'Fashion' competition, and won it several times, though never the main prize, which, I think, used to be a car. No wonder the Press newspaper group went out of business; we sucked them dry.

We grew up in the nuclear age, with the threat of total annihilation hanging over us. It's still there, of course, but we have learned to live with it. It has been largely replaced in our collective consciousness by new fears, like climate change and killer viruses. My mother, in particular, although she was certainly not alone in this, seemed to have a rather unhealthy fascination with the Russians and their apparent need to either take over the world – and in the process destroy the Catholic religion – or indeed, to simply destroy the world. In any case, there was no doubt about the identity of our true enemies – it was the Russians. The issue with Russia was, apparently, not a geopolitical one, or anything like that, it was primarily a question of religion. And so, it could be solved by the power of prayer. In what now sounds like an almost comical touch, at the end of Mass every Sunday, amongst the prayers that were always recited by the priest was one for "the conversion of Russia". By the time I was nine or ten, I had learned enough to know that the cold war was being fought predominantly between the USA and the USSR. I knew about how nuclear radiation could silently and invisibly spread across the globe in the event of nuclear war. Even so, from having studied the map of the world, it was evident that these countries were quite far away from us, and it seemed we should be relatively safe. But, no, Mam maintained, we were far from safe. We lived not too far from Shannon Airport – well, as the crow flies anyway. At night you could see the flashing beacons of the airport light up the sky. That was too close for comfort, she believed. She was convinced that Shannon, an international airport, was one of the first places the Russians would be certain to destroy. Yes, it was a little more strategic then as a stopping-off point for trans-Atlantic flights than it is today, but, even so, her fears were greatly exaggerated. I doubt many Soviet military strategists occupied themselves with how they would firstly nuke Shannon Airport before proceeding to tackle the might of the United States nuclear arsenal. In a strange and frighteningly circular series of events, it now appears that my mother may have been right about the Russians after all. As I write, in April 2022, the Russian invasion of Ukraine is in full swing. Who knows how it will end.

As well as the threat of the nuclear holocaust, the sixties were also dominated by antiwar groups such as CND; the Campaign for Nuclear Disarmament. Right through the decade, they held huge marches and protests in many places around the world, similar to the climate change protest movement of recent years. It was entirely futile, of course. The warmongers carried on as if nothing was happening. I wonder if CND still even exists. One of the interesting things about the lingo that was used at the time was the term "The Bomb". The Bomb did not mean just any old bomb; it meant the atomic bomb. Thus, a very common slogan at these protests was "Ban the Bomb", meaning phase out all nuclear weapons. As a youngster, I knew about "The Bomb" but was inclined to confuse "The Bomb" with bombs in general. Thus, when my older brother James and his first cousin, Dan O'Keeffe, declared that they intended to make their own bomb, I naturally assumed that what they had in mind was a nuclear device. They both considered themselves to be macho, men-of-the-world types, even though they were just teenagers. Also, both of them had a rudimentary interest in things of a scientific nature. In fact, Dan, who later joined the Christian Brothers, went on to become a science teacher. There was an old World War Two spent grenade that had been lying about the place for years. I think it was a leftover from the time when Dad was a volunteer in the Local Defence Forces; a sort of Dad's Army from the early forties. In any case this grenade was to be the container for their bomb – yes, clearly it would have been a little on the petite side for an atomic bomb, but how was I to know? Ingredients would of course consist of the usual recipe of sugar and petrol and perhaps some agricultural fertilizer products; their knowledge of how to produce a massive explosion was minimal, to say the very least of it. The pair of them walked about manfully, discussing military tactics and whatnot. It all appeared very convincing to me, a small boy. I was scared shitless. It was bad enough, what with having to fear the Russians and all, but now, my own brother and our cousin as well! I vividly recall that my mother was getting ready to attend some evening ceremony in the local church. It may have been a First Friday or something of that nature. To my great surprise, despite all her previous warnings about the likelihood of our imminent destruction at the hands of the Russians, she did not appear to be very greatly put out by these activities of a very similar nature, right here on our own doorstep - and with the complicity of her own eldest son, no less. I followed her around, wanting protection, I suppose. Eventually, I asked her right out; "Mam, are they really making a bomb?" Her reply was as shocking as it was frivolous. "Oh, yes, it's true. It seems they are making a bomb alright." I had a tight knot of anxiety in my stomach for the rest of the evening until the pair of them eventually tired of their experimenting and gave up; at least for the time being. After that, the next big problem I had to deal with was the Cuban Missile Crisis of October 1962, the closest the world has come to total destruction from a thermonuclear war. That week, Dad asked me to do some work in the garden. I don't recall exactly what it was, but I do know that I thought "Well, what's the point in doing anything, since we're all going to be burnt alive any day now?" Fortunately, Kennedy and Kruschev reached a deal that took the pressure from me for a while.

The fear of an impending outbreak of hostilities featuring nuclear bombs was so great at the time that the Irish Government of the day even went to the trouble of issuing a booklet on the matter, a copy of which was delivered to every household. It was compiled by the Civil Defence and contained information about what ordinary citizens should do to protect themselves in the event of a nuclear blast, followed by high levels of radioactive fallout. I was fascinated by this publication and read it many times over the following years. Unfortunately, our copy of this document got lost somewhere along the way. However, you can find it online quite easily now. Some of the advice was actually quite sensible, but other sections were simply ludicrous. There were numerous illustrations, the most dramatic of which actually showed a large explosion in the distance. A man is depicted protecting himself by lying on the ground, because apparently one presents less of a target in this position compared to one who is standing upright. Incredibly, the text actually recommends turning one's back to the blast and using an object such as a coat or a briefcase as a protective device. You might think that when the blast is close enough to be clearly visible, then lying on the ground protected by your overcoat is unlikely to afford a great deal of protection. Also, there was advice on how to shelter from the worst of things by retreating into a temporary shelter under the stairs. I was quite concerned about this, as even just a very quick and cursory inspection of the space under our stairs indicated to me that we might as well be living in a bungalow, for all the use it was going to be. The cupboard beneath our stairs was really quite small and was only ever used to store old half-used tins of paint. The very idea of even attempting to cram all eight of us in there just standing up side by side was clearly not on, never mind living in there for a period of time until it was safe to come out again. And even if you did survive that long, then there was the fallout to contend with. While emphasising that fallout is not visible to human sight, its presence was illustrated in the booklet with red spots of dust everywhere. There was even a picture of a farmer handling hay with a hayfork, and in order to minimise his exposure to this deadly killer, he wears a handkerchief over his nose and mouth, and a pair of gloves. No question of a proper facemask, not to mention PPE. I knew that farmer was doomed. I suppose it is easy now to be critical of the almost comical nature of some of the booklet's contents, but, in fairness, it was probably a reasonable attempt to provide at least some very primitive reassurance to the citizens of the nation at the time. It is fascinating to read it again now, although I have often wondered if even a single household in the country adopted any of the advice in relation to the things one could do in advance of an attack, such as, for example, having a large stock of tinned foods set aside. Oh, and candles as well, you were not to forget the candles. We will see you after the half-life of the nuclear fallout will have expired; that should not take more than a few thousand years.

In the 1950's and 1960's, the year 2000 must have seemed almost as far away as the year 2100 does now - I don't know, as I don't even remember thinking about it that far back. Even by the mid-sixties, the end of the twentieth century seemed an impossible distance into the future. It sounds ridiculous now, but pretty much the first thing that we imagined when we thought about moving into a new century was that by then we would all have our own helicopter or airplane. The 1968 movie '2001: A Space Odyssey' only strengthened our expectations, with what can now be seen in retrospect as quite an unrealistic view of space adventures, certainly well more advanced than anything that is likely to be achieved in my lifetime (apart from iPad-like tablets, that feature heavily in the movie). Our biggest hopes for the future were that there would be no more world wars and there would be no more famine, whilst both poverty and disease would be largely banished from human existence. Not too much to ask for, surely, and much of it probably could have been done too, if only priorities had been different. We never even considered anything as awful as a pandemic. Various authorities who came across as being quite smart and fully on top of their brief assured us that nuclear power stations were so safe, there was practically zero possibility of a meltdown ever occurring. Then there were those who predicted that the tedious activities associated with the growing of crops, the rearing of animals and the preparation of food could all be done away with. One would merely swallow a tablet along with a glass of water in the morning, and that would be it, your daily nourishment regimen all taken care of. Also, traditional methods of education would be totally eliminated. There would no longer be any requirement to spend almost the entirety of one's youth attending school after school, since all human knowledge would be simply imbibed by every child soon after birth. By exactly what means this was to be achieved was not clear, but after all, there was still plenty of time to go, more than thirty years, in fact. We were told that man would walk on the moon before 1970, and, sure enough, it did happen. Why would all the other stuff not happen also? Being a fundamentally lazy person, my personal favourite vision for the future was a world where all forms of work would have been eliminated, and we could spend our time simply enjoying ourselves. I was certainly very naively optimistic about the future, but I wasn't the only one. In the sixties it was obvious that various world leaders and their supporters were on the completely wrong track. Nixon, Brezhnev and many others appeared, to me anyway and to many others too, to be nothing less than dangerous demented demagogues. History has proven me right, though, in fairness, you did not need to possess great political nous to see that those guys were just big-time gangsters. I was totally confident that by the time my generation had grown older and having observed how badly things had been handled, well, once our contemporaries would be running the show, everything would be a great deal better. As you may imagine, the older I get, the more disappointed I become. Big-time gangsters they certainly were, but with hindsight it is appalling to have to accept that they now look almost like angels compared to the hideous reality of Trump, Putin, Bolsonaro and various other ignorant, deluded incompetents throughout the world. And the worst of it is that these ignorant, deluded incompetents are **of my generation;** they are **our ignorant, deluded incompetents**. In our most pessimistic projections, we never thought for one moment that things could get this bad. I have to accept the shocking reality; in terms of looking after each other, and the planet we live on, my generation is not just as bad as those that went before, it's actually much worse. So much for progress; if current trends continue, there is little hope for humanity. Imagine if by some scientific miracle we could have seen, in the 1960's, a vision of what the world would be like by the 2020's, complete with ongoing war, poverty, disease, discrimination, crime, injustice and millions of people signing up to crazy religions; perhaps we would have just pleaded with the Americans and the Russians to fire off every nuclear missile at the same time, and just get it all over with quickly.

The neighbouring parish of Shanaglish held an annual sports day, usually, in August, I believe. Over time, the Shanaglish Sports had established itself as a significant day in the calendar for those interested in athletics and cycling. We never missed it, not because we had the slightest interest in athletics, which we did not, but simply because it was a day out, and not too far away from home. The first challenge always was to get in without paying the entry fee. This involved the tracing out of a long and tortuous path through the nearby bushy area, and then attempting to casually slip over the wall into the venue, as though one had merely taken to the undergrowth as a temporary measure to relieve oneself. I believe the entry fee was just a nominal sum, and it would have been a lot easier to simply just pay up, but family tradition and personal pride was at stake. There was a carnival atmosphere around the place, with all the usual roulette wheels, wheels-of-fortune and so on. This is where we spent the day, never even casting as much as a glance at the sporting activities. Once, Francis and I spotted some loose change that had fallen on the ground beside the operator of a roulette table. We well understood all the lessons that had been spelled out over the years about honesty and the right to private property. We soon got over that though, simply by logically deducing that the roulette wheel operator was most likely ripping off the public and therefore had little right to have the money returned to him. We quietly scooped it up and quickly moved away, our consciences perfectly clear once more.

I think I was about nine years old when I began to notice that there were things on the radio that you could actually listen to – prior to that, it had all been just 'noise' to me. In particular, I latched on to music; popular music, not traditional Irish, or classical. It's almost embarrassing to admit it now, but the first pop song I can recall being aware of was 'Sun Arise' by Rolf Harris, of all people. In fairness, it's not a bad song. Not only did I become an avid listener to the weekly 'Top Ten' show on the radio, but major geek that I was, I actually set aside a special notebook, into which I transcribed the details of all the records in the hit parade, as it was called. The notebook was around the place for years, but unfortunately, was eventually lost. I'm pretty sure that one of the presenters was Larry Gogan. Many, many years later, I had the privilege of occasionally working with the same Larry Gogan. He has passed away now, but had such an amazingly long career that not only was he on the radio when I was less than ten years old, he was still broadcasting for some time after I had retired.

I particularly recall having difficulty with the name of a new group, who had a record in the chart for the first time. I had never heard of them, and could not tell how to spell their name. When the DJ announced their name, it sounded like 'The Peetles', or maybe 'The Beedles'. I was not sure what to enter in my precious notebook. My brother Francis came to the rescue. He had read about this new group from Liverpool, who were becoming famous for their music and their long hair. Before long, I was a major fan, and have been ever since.

There were some past-times or hobbies that I just never got into, such as stamp-collecting or having a pen-friend. My sisters did indulge themselves in some of those activities, and perhaps they were seen as more suited for girls. This was a time when boys mostly did boys things and girls mostly did girls things. Gender equality was generations away. It didn't stop me from reading girls' comic books though. I consumed all comics voraciously, regardless of what their target market was. So I knew well who Cotter, Field, Radleigh and Simpson were. Do you? I also used to indulge myself in sneaking a look at my sisters' stamp albums in a failed effort to figure out what the attraction of it all was. Admittedly, when a new consignment of stamps arrived in the post, it was always kind of interesting to look through them. They did look a lot more colourful and exotic than our own Irish variety. A strange custom existed relating to postage stamps that arrived on the envelopes of letters from our relatives in the USA, India and so on. My mother always tore off the corner of the envelope bearing the stamp. For whatever reason, one did not actually remove the stamp on its own; it had to be left still attached to a piece of the envelope – why I do not know. These stamps she kept in a tin box on the mantelpiece above the range in the kitchen. When asked what the purpose of keeping the stamps was, she always maintained that it was something to do with helping 'the missions'. As far as I know, nothing was ever done with the tin of stamps. It may still be there. The only kind of stamps I ever collected was Post Office savings stamps. Any time you were sent to the Post Office you were permitted, or indeed even encouraged, to use the change to purchase one savings stamp; they cost sixpence each. That's 6d, one-fortieth of a pound. It took a very long time to accumulate even one pound in savings. Over a period of ten years or more, I did save a few quid. Then one day in my teens, I took it all out and spent it. And what did I treat myself to? I don't even remember.

The Post Office had a very old-fashioned telephone system that was completely manually driven – there was no public call box. If you needed to use a telephone, you either had to go to a neighbour who had one, and very few had, or go to the Post Office, and have the lady there put the call through for you. Many phone calls were for 'Clarecastle'. This needs clarification. We did not simply make calls, as such, to Clarecastle, which is a village near the town of Ennis. In, or perhaps close to Clarecastle, there was a set-up devoted specifically to making cows pregnant, via artificial insemination. This is not a joke. The institution may even still exist, for all I know. Presumably, they somehow extracted the necessary ingredient from their collection of bulls. I do not care to even speculate as to how one might go about achieving such an outcome. When a phone call came from a farmer indicating that a cow required the relevant attention, 'the man from Clarecastle' would subsequently arrive on site, equipped with the necessary tubes containing the 'right stuff'. There was no mistaking the car, as these guys always drove a white Volkswagen Beetle. It was a most undesirable type of job and I cannot imagine why anybody would want to do it. Actually, a lot of the activities that occur on a cattle farm can be quite graphic in nature. Years ago, when we were growing up, all cattle had a large pair of horns on their heads. From the seventies or so onwards, none of them did. How do you think the change came about? Well, it's not through evolution, I can tell you that. And why are all bullocks not bulls? Think about it. From an early age, I knew that I would never want to have anything to do with working close to animals. Observing what vets and the fellows from Clarecastle had to do for a living just further reinforced my convictions in this regard.

One of the hobbies that I did attempt to indulge myself in was collecting model cars. Everybody wore leather shoes for 'good wear' - which meant for Mass on Sunday. Our shoes always had to be polished for this occasion, and the polish we used was called 'Nugget'. It came in a small flat round tin. In an attempt to sell even more tins of the stuff, the Nugget manufacturing organisation offered miniature models of various popular cars at a reduced price, as long as you could send them proof of purchase. I really wanted these models, but, frustratingly, the tins of Nugget polish seemed to last forever and we never seemed to have enough of them to qualify for the offer. When I drew my mother's attention to this apparent deficit in our domestic arrangements, she completely understood my requirements and pretty quickly made the necessary adjustment; that is to say, she went and bought enough tins of Nugget shoe-polish to last us for a couple of years. I was able to send away for the model cars that I desired. They duly arrived in the post and I had them for years. They were made of real metal, you could open and close the bonnet *and* you could remove and put back on the tyres. Clockwork toys were also prevalent before battery-operated devices took over. We had various clockwork toys, but the best one ever was a miniature motorbike, complete with rider, that I got one Christmas. When you wound it up, it would go round and round in circles. It may sound boring, but it was beautifully made and I loved it. Sadly, I did not have it for very long. In a dreadful error of judgment I took it to school after the Christmas holidays to show to one of my fellow pupils. He saw how attractive it was and immediately demanded to know 'how much I wanted for it'. I did not want to sell it at all, but in an act of foolishness or weakness or whatever, I let him talk me into accepting ten shillings for the little bike. Ten shillings, half of a pound or the equivalent of 50 pence in later times, was an enormous amount of cash for a small boy in the early 1960's. I simply did not know what to do with such riches. Also, I did not want any of my family to know that I had parted with the lovely motorbike that I had just so recently received from Santy. I soon realised that the money was of little practical use to me, as I could not do anything with it. What could I spend it on, without drawing attention to the fact that I had parted with my one of my own favourite toys? So I did the only thing that I could do in the circumstances – I told nobody anything. I placed the crisp orange-coloured ten-shilling note carefully in the breast pocket of the jacket I wore only to Mass on Sunday mornings. Nobody would ever find it there – I thought. In any case, I reasoned to myself, I would eventually grow old enough to spend it. Some weeks later, on a Sunday morning, we were about to set out for the local church. We were a big family in a small car, and, as was the custom at the time, we children were literally 'stacked up' in the back seat. I don't believe that seat belts had even been invented. The smaller children had to sit on their older and larger siblings' laps. I was seated on the lap of my older brother, Francis. Looking over my shoulder, and availing of his excellent vision, he spotted the ten-shilling note that was not really very well hidden in my jacket breast pocket. Whipping it out, he held it up and waved it around for all to see, whilst announcing to the world; 'Johnny has money!' My mother immediately instigated a full and serious investigation into the entire matter, the upshot being that I was told I would have to return the rather large sum of money to my colleague at school. I reluctantly did so, hoping that I would then get my clockwork motorbike back. I never saw it again.

The 1960's saw a slight improvement in the standard of living for many people in Ireland, due, we are told, to greater industrialisation. One of the more obvious ways in which this manifested itself was that many local families, indeed most of them, acquired a car for the first time. In many cases they actually purchased a brand new car, not just second-hand. In the course of a few years, we went from being one of the very few families that owned a car at all, to being one that had a car that was generally much older and thus less reliable than those of our immediate neighbours. My mother didn't care for that at all. There was no driving test at the time, and it has to be said that the standard of driving was often rather poor. Consequently, road accident statistics for the sixties and seventies are truly shocking by today's standards. Even new cars were far from perfect, and certainly did not compare to today's super-comfortable and super-reliable machines. I clearly recall a neighbouring family who took a trip every Sunday in their shiny Morris Minor. The grown son, Tommy, drove his parents on these outings. Where they went we never knew, or never asked. Before embarking on this weekly voyage, Tommy would drive the car on his own, half a mile or so over the road, passing by our house on the way over and again on the way back, before taking his parents on board. The purpose of this little "mini-trip" was apparently by way of "testing" the car, as preparation for the forthcoming journey – which was probably going to be no more than a few miles anyway. This was a time when one could still pretty reliably identify every single car that passed by. Yes, it was a rather remote place. If you happened to glance out the window on a Sunday afternoon and observe Tommy's "pre-flight routine", one was expected to inform all and sundry; "There's Tommy now - testing". Not much went by unnoticed. My mother claimed that she personally witnessed another neighbouring young man flip his van upside-down almost right outside our front entrance. Alas, such excitement was extremely rare.

From a young age Francis was big into fishing, so much so that our Dad built a small wooden jetty at the side of the river for him and for my other brother James. The pair of them often caught many fish there, mostly roach and perch. As the younger brother, in time I naturally felt the pressure was on me to follow suit. The bait of choice was live worms. Being a major wimp, I had great difficulty in even handling these horrible wriggly things, and as for impaling one on a fish-hook, that really was an experience never to be repeated. Hardened anglers will tell you that a worm is a very crude and undeveloped species and that they possess no nerves at all and thus can feel no pain. That's not how it looked, and felt, to me. From what I remember, my fishing career began and ended on the same day.

In later years, Francis built small flat-bottomed rowing boats from marine plywood and we regularly went up and down the same stretch of river in these. Looking out over the side of the boat into the black depths of the water certainly puts your faith in a sibling's woodworking skills to the test. Not one of those boats ever leaked as much as a drop.

Francis started out catching roach and perch in the Moyrhee River, but as the years went by, he significantly developed his angling skills and progressed on to fly fishing for trout and salmon. After successful evenings of trout fishing in various nearby rivers, he would gut and clean out the fish, ready for cooking the following morning. There is really no better breakfast than fresh trout. Salmon is always regarded as the crème de la crème of freshwater fish, but I always preferred the trout. Francis knew exactly where the fish were located in the local rivers, and he knew how to catch them. Very occasionally, I accompanied him on these expeditions. I found it almost impossible to get my head around the extreme degree of patience that is required of an angler. Most of the time, the fisherman catches nothing. The really interesting aspect of that, of course, is that the consistent angler does not regard such lack of catch as any kind of failure; he sees it rather as more of an eminently satisfying way to have passed a fine evening, whilst the business of actually putting fish in the bag is really just an occasional bonus. I often stood on a river bank with Francis as he pointed out various fish that he was keeping a close eye on in the water. Usually I could see nothing, and even when I did just about manage to make out the dark slippery-looking shapes of the fish moving about, I marvelled at his eyesight and his ability to detect and track such elusive prey. I particularly recall one very warm summer evening when we went to a small lake surrounded by bogland in a mountainy place. After fifteen minutes or so, I realised I was being eaten alive – by midges. I have never encountered so many voracious blood-sucking insects anywhere, before or since. I had to run back to the car for shelter, and sit there itching and scratching in the sweltering heat until Francis returned, hours later - without any fish, of course. When I asked him how he was able to withstand the ceaseless air war that was conducted by the human-hating insects, he just replied, 'Midges? What midges?'

Francis was always closer to nature than any of us and probably still is. He even went to the trouble of having a load of gravel dumped into a shallow section of the river, thus creating a suitable environment for local fish to bask in. He would even dispense food to them from the riverbank. Essentially, he had created his own enormous fish-tank – except that the fish were free to come and go as they pleased. A fish-hotel, you might say. He could make pets of young calves also. I witnessed him holding a chunk of turnip sticking out of his mouth and have a calf come forward and take it from him. I have never seen anyone else perform a feat quite like that.

We had various other adventures on the river. My mother was a member of the local guild of the ICA (Irish Countrywomens Association). At one point, they decided they would undertake the practice of weaving, using dried reeds. These reeds grew in profusion on the banks of the river that flowed through our land. I cannot even say what they intended to construct at their weaving sessions, perhaps baskets or something. I took no interest in the activities of the ICA, until my mother mentioned that they were prepared to pay sixpence for every bunch of fifty reeds. Riches were to be had! That summer I spent many days standing on the bank of the river with a scythe, cutting many hundreds and hundreds of reeds. I worked within inches of water so deep it was totally black to the eye. Nobody could see me where I worked, and had I taken one false step, it would have been all over for me. The lure of money is certainly a driving force to be reckoned with. I only made a few pounds from my work, and I have forgotten how I spent it, but at least I escaped with my life.

One evening, when my mother had just returned from a meeting of the ICA, as mentioned above, she proceeded to relate the news of the evening. Of course, I am not suggesting for one moment that ICA meetings were simply a gossip-fest, but let's just say that she always had lots to tell upon her return from one of these regular events. I never paid the slightest bit of attention, since this was all adult stuff that was of little interest to me. On this particular occasion though, things turned out to be different. She mentioned that a teacher of traditional Irish music had been engaged to call to the parish hall on one evening a week, in order to give lessons to the local children. Then I happened to overhear her say; "And Johnny will go". This was how such matters were negotiated and communicated. I had no interest at all in learning to play Irish music. Despite being rather stubborn in nature, I suppose I must have been relatively easy to control all the same. I went. It was a disaster. The very first evening, I arrived at the hall, equipped with my older brother James' tin whistle. There must have been a dozen other youngsters there. And without exception, every single one of them was festooned with a large accordion. Perhaps my mother had not been fully paying attention when that element of the music lessons was under discussion, I don't know. In any case, I stuck it for a few weeks. In between each weekly lesson, I dutifully attempted to learn the assigned piece of music. They were mostly fairly simple Irish melodies and I could learn to play them off by heart. That's not to say there was any heart in the way I played them, because there was not. Eventually, a week came when the piece we were given to learn was quite a difficult one, and I simply failed to beat it into shape. Each weekly session always began with the entire group of so-called musicians playing the latest piece all together. On this occasion, I simply blew random notes on my instrument, hoping that I could get away with it. The good thing about being the only tin whistle player amongst a large group of accordions was that I could not be heard in the midst of the dreadful cacophony. Or so I thought. The music teacher clearly had a much keener ear than I had hitherto suspected, for he came to me immediately and asked if I had learned the piece at all. I was frozen to the spot at first, but then went on the defensive right away, insisting that I had indeed learned it. I don't know why I did that, instantly realising I had set a very obvious trap for myself, and that his next clear move would be to dare me to play it on my own. To my surprise, he did not behave like a typical teacher at all. Displaying remarkable control and declining to subject me to the ritual type of humiliation one habitually expected from people in his position, he simply walked away and moved on to the next stage of that week's session. I'd had enough though. I determined that I would never go back and find myself in such a situation again. I had learned very little, and finally requested my mother to release me from bondage. To my surprise, she relented immediately. Maybe it was the case that no longer having to listen to my pathetic efforts at attempting to play the instrument came as something of a relief to the entire family.

Early Teenage Years

When I first started secondary school in the town of Gort in 1965, there was no bus transport for school pupils. I cycled to school, like everybody else. It was nine miles each way. This may sound like a lot, especially for a twelve-year-old; and it was. But there were others who travelled by bike from beyond Kinvara, in some cases covering up to thirteen miles to get to Gort. I will say it made one fit. By the time I was in second year, I sometimes cycled to school and back and then later on the same evening, cycled back to Gort again to attend the cinema. I remember seeing the early Clint Eastwood so-called 'dollars movies' or 'spaghetti westerns' in this way. The really satisfying part of this was that the school pupils who lived in the town of Gort were required to attend after-school study every evening, not finishing until 9 PM. Three hours of that every school evening for the full five years! Of course, those of us who lived out in the countryside could not be expected to do this, thus we got away scot-free, as it were, just doing the amount of study that suited us. So, while I was in the cinema enjoying the latest escapades of 'The Man with no Name', or whatever, my townie schoolmates were just a couple of hundred yards further up the street, stuck inside in the school that was patrolled by prowling priests. The bit none of us could escape though was Saturday school. Yes, we were required to attend for a half-day on every Saturday of the school year. It was a ridiculous arrangement; obviously the few classes we had on a Saturday morning could have easily been integrated into the Monday to Friday schedule, simply by extending the hours a little bit. But that would have been too easy. The entire system seemed to be geared towards making our secondary school experience as harsh and unpleasant as it could possibly be. I suppose the teachers must have hated it too, although it has to be said that their welfare was the last thing on our minds. Even in the conventional workplace, the working week was in the process of being reduced to a five-day arrangement. The other thing that is also long forgotten now is that, until the mid-sixties, the old-age pension did not apply until seventy years of age. Recent attempts to increase the retirement age from 66 back up towards 70 envisage quite a reversal of the progressive trends of the 1960's. I would not be surprised if the six-day week working were to make a comeback too.

My older sister Gerita attended boarding school for the full five years. The convent school in question was also in Gort - the same town where I attended day-school. Occasionally, my mother would give me a package to be delivered to Gerita. I believe these packages contained food; it was well understood that the unfortunate boarders were not overfed. I accomplished the delivery by simply hanging the parcel on the large doorknob on the front door of the convent – there was no human interaction involved. The convent door was directly across the street from the school I attended, the two buildings being separated by a distance of no more than a few yards, really. Yet, the system was so inhumane and devoid of any semblance of normality, that, not only did I never actually get to see my own sister, I encountered no human being at all. I suppose what was even worse was that I took it all for granted – that was just the way it was. My younger sister, Rose, was also sent to boarding school in Kinvara, for three years. She subsequently attended day-school in Gort. By that time, bus transport for secondary school pupils had been introduced. This still necessitated a journey of about three miles from our house just to get to the bus stop; a lot easier than the full nine miles though.

Once every month (unless my memory deceives me it was always the first Tuesday) a cattle-fair was held in the town of Gort. Cattle were bought and sold all over the town, right there on the footpaths outside the shop-doors. By the time we got out for lunch, the entire town was literally swimming in fresh cow-dung and urine. Living and rearing animals in the heart of the countryside is a dirty business of course, but somehow it always seemed so much worse on the streets of the town. Shopkeepers spread sheets of cardboard and newspaper at their entrances but their efforts were in vain really – customers brought the muck on their boots into the shops, and we brought it back into school. The upside was that travelling hawkers set up their stands in the square, selling various agricultural supplies to the farmers visiting town for the day. And they also sold something that we youngsters valued highly – stink bombs. These came in a tiny glass container – almost like a little miniature bottle. Crush the little container, and the evil genie was out of the bottle. The stink on the streets and footpaths was already quite something, but this was on another level altogether. I don't know what the liquid inside was constituted from, but it lived up to its name – the stink was truly disgusting. The thing was to let it off and move away quickly. Once, somebody let one off in the school classroom, and even though it was a very large room, it was almost more than we could bear for the entire afternoon.

Apart from holidays, Sundays and when you were genuinely sick, there were also rare days when you would be let stay away from school. This was when there was such important and pressing farm work to be done that a day off from school was called for. One such event was delivering cattle to the mart. This involved a very early start. The actual mart itself was very boring for me as I really had no interest in the proceedings there. It could take hours before our animals were auctioned off. The good part was that Dad would give me a few shillings for comics and sweets. Unlike now, where the cattle marts are always located outside the town, back then they were always centrally situated. This was very convenient for my important shopping expeditions. When we finally got back home, my mother was always predictably disappointed with the prices the cattle had fetched.

A good few years later, Francis and I witnessed a distressing sight associated with the cattle mart in the town of Ennis. Two men were bringing a large herd of animals from the mart to where their cattle-truck was parked, a few hundred yards away. They ran the cattle at full speed down the road – something that should never be done. For one unfortunate bullock, the experience was just too much. It collapsed to the ground, and, right away, it was quite evident to us that the beast had expired. The two men carried on, leaving the animal where it had fallen. It was one of the cruellest things I have ever witnessed. Worse was to come. Shortly after, one of the ignorant brutes returned to the scene of the crime, and in a frenzied display of anger and frustration, he set about lashing the dead animal's body with a large stick, cursing and swearing and urging it to get back up off the ground. On more than one occasion I have witnessed a cattle-farmer crying genuine tears, following the unexpected death of one of their herd. That fellow on the streets of Ennis had the bearing of a man who would not cry even after the death of a family member.

Christmas

I enjoy Christmas Day just like anybody else. But as for everything Christmas-related that goes on prior to that date, beginning, it would seem, as early as September, well, I could easily do without a lot of it. I used to think that made me an isolated curmudgeon, but I am finding that more and more people are in agreement with me. So, I'm not an isolated curmudgeon after all, I'm simply another quietly suffering curmudgeon; one amongst many.

What do we find most annoying about the so-called 'pre-Christmas' period? Oh, and, by the way, is not the entire year "pre-Christmas"? Almost everyone will point to the relentless barrage of media commercials and marketing, the non-stop aural and visual diarrhoea-like stream of "Buy, Buy, Buy" that occupies almost every inch of available space for sale on TV, radio, cinema, online and in printed publications. 'But you don't have to look at any of that stuff if you don't like it', you may well respond. And it's true that I don't like much of it. Actually, I despise a great deal of it. But how can I avoid it? I mean, it's everywhere, isn't it? There are millions of us out there, and when I say "us", I mean "us curmudgeons", or, should that be "we curmodgeons"? Now, just imagine if we were to get organised and to arrange ourselves in a pressure group, a kind of United Nations of "Let's-keep-Christmas-until-Christmas-Eve-at- the-earliest". It's not a very catchy title, I grant you that, but I'm sure any of those experts who design the much-admired Christmas advertising campaigns for John Lewis, M&S and so on, could be prevailed upon to develop an appropriate (and brief) title. With the power of numbers behind us, we could surely persuade the governments of the world to make all reference to Christmas-related produce illegal before, say, December 15th – yes, I would prefer if they held off until Christmas Eve, but one has to be prepared to compromise in such matters. It's probably best not to mention the Christian concept of Advent at all, since this season begins between November 27 and December 3 – far too early, in my view.

Hallowe'en was an annual seasonal event that was relatively low-key compared to Christmas. These days the build-up to Hallowe'en begins part way through September. The event itself has been entirely transformed, especially in recent decades, with much attendant so-called 'trick or treating' as well as children dressing up in an array of very elaborate costumes. It is all entirely unrecognisable compared to the Hallowe'en of our day, and I have to say that, in my opinion, it is greatly improved. That's not to say we did not celebrate it, because we certainly did, but in very different ways, ways that probably seem rather tame and underwhelming by comparison. We did our best to convince ourselves that witches, ghouls and so on were actually free to roam the land for one truly scary night. Once, I did my best to put all this into a poem, the words of which I have unfortunately forgotten, bar the first two lines;

'Tonight is the night of all nights,

When witches and goblins are out'.

There were several verses, but you will have to make them up for yourself. Be sure to attend carefully to the meter, and also remember that it must rhyme properly; those things were quite important to me. Our parents always provided a selection of nuts, including walnuts, almonds, monkey nuts and, of course, hazelnuts that grew in profusion locally. The nutcracker was hauled out of its location in a drawer of the kitchen dresser, and heavily used for the evening. It would not see the light of day again for a year. My mother disapproved of anyone using their teeth to crack a nut, though she was quite prepared to admit that she had destroyed her own set of teeth with the same practice, as well as through consuming large quantities of hard toffee. There was always a brack, with the requisite ring inside it. But we had never even heard of 'trick or treating'. There was no 'dressing up'. Nobody ever went to another's house; it was entirely a home event. We played all the old-fashioned games that are largely forgotten now, such as trying to pick up coins from inside a basin of water, using only your mouth. There was an incentive to try hard at this; if you could manage to pick up some of the money, then you could keep it. Snap-apple was a perennial favourite, of course. And then, wearing a blindfold while you reached out to choose one from a selection of saucers that contained objects such as a ring, water, money, dirt etc, indicating that you were to be married, or to travel across the sea, or to become rich or even to die. Of course, you just kept going until you got the answer you really wanted. The real highlight of the evening though, for me anyway, was 'Blind Man's Buff'. The kitchen was cleared with the table pushed back to the side of the room. One person at a time was blindfolded and had the apparently simple task of groping around to try and grab hold of someone, anyone, that person then assuming the role of the blindfolded one. It is a very simple exercise, almost primitive in nature, but I have rarely enjoyed any other game as much in my life. Hiding and escaping from the temporarily blinded 'hunter' was always tremendously exciting for me, and I was good at it, rarely being 'caught'. The best fun, of course, was creeping up behind the one in the blindfold, tapping and teasing them in an effort to intensify their frustration. If they happened to hear you approaching from behind, there was always the danger that they would swiftly turn and grab you; in those circumstances, you had to be prepared to 'run for your life', as it were. Sooner or later though, one was inevitably caught, and I was always a little bit terrified when the blindfold went on me, even though I knew perfectly well that it was just a temporary measure. It does present a very rough idea of what it must be like to actually lose your vision, and I was always intensely relieved when I could finally relinquish the blindfold, having caught somebody else. That somebody else was often my mother, and I believe now that she deliberately put herself in the way of being caught somewhat easily, rather than let the unfortunate blindfolded one wander around in a daze, becoming more and more disorientated. All too soon, Hallowe'en was over and done with, in one short evening. But they were evenings that I have never forgotten and I never will; they were simply wonderful.

For us children, the Christmas season began in earnest the day the school term ended and the holidays began. On the afternoon of the final day at school, the teacher produced a gigantic box of sweets. Well, it looked gigantic to us. They were usually "Lemons Pure Sweets", a brand that, I regret to say, has been extinct for many decades now. Each sweet had the word "Lemons" embossed upon it and each one resembled a tiny bar of soap. Not in taste, of course. The flavour varied with the colour. They were hard and semi-transparent. And they were lovely to suck on. Even the paper in which each sweet was individually wrapped was like a tiny piece of colourful art. The sweets were doled out to us, and, it has to be said, it was done in a manner that was fair to all, regardless of one's past record in academic performance, or one's general behaviour. This practice was also observed at the beginning of the summer holidays. It appears to have been more than just a custom; it almost had the status of an obligatory event. Why did the teacher suddenly behave in this bizarre manner? Over the full course of the term that was just ending, she would have punished us physically from time to time, and berated us verbally on a daily basis. The milk of human kindness was in very short supply ninety-nine per cent of the time. We were left in no doubt that we were all really quite stupid and incapable of being taught the most trivial lesson. Then in one brief, albeit entirely predictable, departure from the norm, here she was, handing out sweets to all and sundry. There was no accounting for it, though of course, we did not question it either. I suppose the kindest way to consider the matter is to assume that the entire business of attempting to teach us anything at all was such a tremendously frustrating experience for the teacher that, much of the time, she simply could not conceal her rage. For, rage she did, and often. And then, at last, the holidays! Now, I suppose, she could behave in the benevolent way that she always wanted to but was unable to. Now that is really giving her the benefit of the doubt. The contrast with how things are done today could hardly be greater. On the day of the holidays now, it is the pupils who bring gifts of sweets and chocolates to the teacher. Even by the 1970's things had already changed a lot. My older sister Gerita was by then herself a teacher in a secondary school. At the end of term some of her students had given her cards and I remember seeing one that read "To Miss Brew, my favourite teacher". In the '60's, we would never have considered even saying thanks to a teacher, never mind write it on a card. If anybody had suggested that we should express appreciation for all that our teachers did for us, I expect we would have replied "Well, they get paid to teach us, don't they?" A bit like the Bash St. Kids, whose famous complaint was "We do all the work and the teacher gets paid!"

Despite all the above, let me be clear; as a child, I loved Christmas. It was definitely my favourite time of the year, bar none. And, what's more, I also liked the lead up to Christmas; the part I favour the least now. Perhaps it is the years that have made me bitter, rather than the onslaught of commercial pressure. Some will say that the commercial pressure has always been there – and that is true, but only partly so. I have been witnessing Christmasses now since the early 1950's. Thus, I declare myself to be an expert; this current season is my seventieth, after all. And, yes, advertising was always a part of Christmas - of course it was. What has altered is the degree of it, the sheer bulk and powerful drive of it all, the overwhelming nature of the beast. In fact, the irony of it is that, as a youngster in the '50's and '60's, I anticipated Christmas so eagerly, my complaint then was that there was actually not enough mention of it in the lead up to the event itself. For example, where I grew up, the local weekly newspaper, the "Clare Champion", referred to by all as simply 'the Champion", might feature a few small representations of the head of Santa Claus, along with a few tiny holly leaves, in some of its advertising. Just in black and white, mind you; most newspapers were printed only in black and white then. Later on, the "Sunday Press", the premier Sunday paper of the time, began to feature a crude element of colour in some of its advertisements – the excitement! I was amused recently to hear that there were objections to a potato crisp maker using the word "crispness" in an effort to convince shoppers that Christmas would not be complete without an adequate supply of its product. For potato crisp aficionados of my generation, this is nothing new – Tayto featured the slogan "Happy Crispness" in its ads in the Sunday Press, and elsewhere, back in the '60's. (The crisp-maker's other not-so-slick slogan of the time was "often imiTaytoed, never equalled"). Perhaps you may wonder how I could possibly recall such detail, bearing in mind I sometimes experience difficulty recalling what happened yesterday. The answer is that only somebody who was a newspaper geek would remember such things. Yes, I was a newspaper geek. Of course, the term did not exist back then. Indeed, I do not believe the word "geek" itself had yet been born, but I was one anyway. When I picked up a daily paper, I read things that most people never saw, like the volume number and the edition number. Many papers then featured a small blank area in the bottom left hand corner of the front page. This was set aside for "Late News". As I understood it, this area could be filled in after the main printing job was complete. It was invariably empty, and on the very rare occasion when something was printed there, reporting for example, an exploding volcano in some distant exotic location, my excitement knew no bounds. By contrast, I did not take a great deal of interest in the actual general news content; that was largely boring. The reproduction of photographs (all black and white, of course) was sometimes so poor that, with careful observation, you could actually discern the individual black, white and various shades of grey dots of which the photo was constituted; very roughly the equivalent of today's pixels. I was fascinated by that; how could anybody not be? It would be many years later before I discovered that these photographs could be delivered over international communications links, literally dot by dot. How satisfying it is to know that.

Talking of newspaper photographs, here is a detail that only a true geek would know. It doesn't really have any direct relationship to Christmas, but it was in November, so, by today's standards, that would be close enough. The date in question is November 23rd, 1963. To anyone of my generation, that is an instantly recognisable date; the day after John F. Kennedy was assassinated. This event was overwhelmingly shocking to most Irish families, to such a degree that my family did something that, to my knowledge, they had never done before, and never did again. They purchased a copy of the Irish Press (my parents were both de Valera admirers so this was something they did every weekday), AND a copy of the Irish Independent. Perhaps there still was a vain hope that at least one of the papers would report that the entire thing was some kind of sick joke, and, with any luck, Kennedy was alive and well, and ready to continue representing Ireland and Catholicism in the White House. This, apparently, was how many Irish people believed he occupied himself. In any case, buying more than one daily paper was quite unheard of. In normal circumstances, the Independent (regarded by my parents as a Fine Gael rag) would only be acquired if the Press was unavailable due to a strike or some similar act of God. Even then, the Cork Examiner would be preferred, if it could be got. The Irish Times was completely out of the question, generally regarded as being only for pretentious snobs; many shops did not even carry the Times. On the day in question, I was sent to the shop for the papers – my favourite kind of mission. Both papers had the same headline: "PRESIDENT KENNEDY ASSASSINATED" in banner headlines. I loved banner headlines; they were rare and I knew they were reserved for extremely significant events, so that was exciting. But beneath the headlines, the two papers revealed a striking contrast. Each paper had printed exactly the same photo, showing the scene in the Presidential open-topped limousine just prior to the actual event. No doubt, the photo had arrived on "the wires", as described above, and from the same photographic agency, but there was a major difference; one paper showed the scene as if the car were travelling from left to right; the other showed it in the opposite direction. For me, the big mystery of the day was not "Who shot Kennedy?", but, rather, how did the two newspaper publishers manage to get the same picture the opposite way around? Of course, there all sorts of technical reasons for how it could have occurred. I have wondered about it ever since. Such is the life of a newspaper geek. I even found myself scanning through each Sunday's copy of 'The Irish Catholic', possibly the most boring paper ever published. I never found as much as a single item of interest in it.

I was so fascinated with newspapers but at the same time so unimpressed by much of their content that, at about the age of ten or so, I resolved to rectify the situation by publishing my own weekly paper, to be known as 'The Tubber Star'. I was the publisher, editor, reporter and everything rolled into one. I possessed a primitive printing kit that was so laborious to deploy, it was easier to just use pen and paper. I could only manage a few pages, most of it consisting of made-up lies and speculation. The circulation never exceeded just one copy, and it was only available within our own household. The slogan across the top of the front page read 'Biggest sale in Moyrhee. Best for scandals'. Based on the usual preoccupation with making easy money, I tried to turn a profit by charging each member of the family sixpence, but most of them never paid up. It ran on that basis for a few years, so, guys, don't forget – you owe me, big time. I even had a go at drawing my own cartoon strip called 'Laughing Larry'. Despite my best efforts, the cartoons never looked terribly impressive. It would be many years before I figured out the reason for that. It turns out the reason is quite simple and rather obvious; I am unable to draw. One of the biggest problems I initially encountered was simply finding adequate quantities of blank paper to write on. As usual, Dad came to the rescue. When he was out and about, he would always call into a shop somewhere and bring me home a few sheets of paper, known as 'foolscap', a bit larger than A4. I don't know if such a thing even still exists. He never let me down. The Tubber Star came out every Sunday, no matter what. I don't know what became of all the copies of the paper. Perhaps they were used to get the fire going.

Christmas was the only time of the year that we ever had in our house, what might be now described as a 'party', though we would never have called it that. The evening did not carry any sort of title; it was merely a night coming up to Christmas when some relatives and friends would be invited to come and have dinner. It was one of the few times in the year that the 'good room' or 'parlour' was actually put to use, other than as a sort of 'playroom' for us kids. Now Christmas was truly under way. A local family, the Mulkeres, well-known in the world of traditional music, nearly always showed up. My mother would greet them with the usual inquiry, "By any chance, did ye bring any instruments with ye?" Feigning surprise, one of them would inevitably reply, "Oh, sure, we'll go back out and have a look in the boot of the car. There might just be something in there." And moments later, they would return, laden down with musical instruments. Their amazing singing and playing abilities really made the evening.

Many seasonal traditions that were then regarded as sacrosanct are forgotten now; at least to some degree. For example, candles were lit on Christmas Eve and one put in each window of the house, facing the road. However, no candles were put in the windows to the rear of the house, except perhaps one in the kitchen. I suppose the thinking was that if a wandering stranger were to arrive looking for a place to stay, they would almost certainly approach from the road. But, I sometimes wondered, what if they were really badly lost and arrived via the overgrown territory to the rear of our house? They might not notice any candle-lit window, and would surely pass by, assuming they were not welcome, even on Christmas Eve. The really peculiar part of this practice was that the first candle was always lit by the youngest boy in the household – and that happened to be me. Why the youngest? Why a boy? Why not the oldest girl? There were six of us and the gender divide was equal; three of each. To my knowledge, not one of my three sisters ever questioned this. Neither did either of my two older brothers; though I have to assume they must have had their opportunity before I came along and took over. I did not question it either. Year in and year out, I went along with this custom, never refusing it, never offering to let somebody else do it for a change. My mother led to me to believe that lighting the Christmas Eve candle was a rather important function, and one with religious significance. And in those times, what could be more important? I suppose I was very pleased with myself, and it was easy to get carried away with the whole spirit and maybe even the power of the occasion. Selflessness was not part of it, apparently. They do say power always corrupts, don't they?

These days, it is fashionable to light candles all over the house at any old time of the year, but, as far as I can recall, candles were never lit at any time other than Christmas. It was such a rare thing to have lighted candles in the bedroom windows, it made my mother fearful that the curtains would catch fire. So, one of us, and for some reason it was usually me, would be sent around to the rooms every half-an-hour or so on a kind of '"fire patrol". That made me feel important, although I don't know what I would have done if I'd actually been faced with a room on fire. Also, it was customary to light a fire in at least one of the bedrooms – these old houses were fitted with a fireplace in each bedroom, even if the fire was rarely lit. Why did it seem to be a good idea to light a fire in a bedroom on Christmas Eve in particular? I do not know. All I do know is that it lent even more self-importance to my routine fire patrol.

"Decorating", now that must have been a tedious custom - for my Dad anyway. There was an unwritten but equally inviolable law that every house must be "decorated" in the weeks coming up to Christmas. "Decorating" did not mean hanging tinsel and so on, although that had to be done too. No, it meant wallpapering and painting; we would call it re-decorating now. However, it was not quite as demanding as it sounds, since "decorating the house" really meant decorating the kitchen only. The kitchen of every country house was where all human life unfolded; the other rooms were little more than places to sleep, and thus were given little attention by comparison. I do not recall any other room in the house ever being repainted or repapered. Just as well for my Dad, particularly when it came to wallpapering; that was his domain. This work was always carried out in the evening-time, as Dad would be occupied with farm-work during the day. Any farmer who valued his reputation would not wish to be seen conducting such unmanly type activity during normal working daylight hours – but after darkness had fallen, well, apparently that was alright. Like many similar houses, ours was quite old and suffered from a degree of dampness. It seems there was no such thing as a damp-proof course back in the day. The heat from the kitchen range that hardly ever went out was enough to keep the place dry most of the time. Nevertheless, in the course of a year, some of the wallpaper from the previous pre-Christmas decorating season would have peeled away from the wall. So, the first task was to remove this and clean up the surface in preparation for the new stuff. In the course of doing so, it would often happen that wallpaper going back years would be revealed, layer upon layer, like an onion. The excitement was tremendous; "Oh, do you remember that pattern? I'd completely forgotten we had such awful-looking wallpaper in 1962!"

Like any bunch of typical youngsters, we scampered around the room while the job was progressing, hugely enjoying the gradual transformation of our environment. My older brother James, though, was far too serious to get involved in our high jinks. In the evenings, it was his custom to settle himself with a library book, and he rarely lifted his head from it, other than to occasionally deliver a remark at us, such as "What's all the noise about?", when we became just a little too boisterous. We would momentarily freeze, like a paused video game, only to resume normal activities as soon as we observed that his head was safely back in the book. I believe it was all a bit of an act on his part though, because when I got to know him better in later years, I began to learn he was no more serious a character than myself; perhaps even less so. I observed him carry this charade to a remarkable degree during one typical winter's evening of wallpapering, an activity in which he took no interest whatsoever. All evening long, while utter chaos ensued all around him, he sat in his chair in the middle of the kitchen, library book held up close to his face, assiduously immersed in an account of civil war in Kenya or whatever his current interest happened to be. He did not lift his gaze from the book until about 11 PM or so. Then he put the book down, looked around the room for a moment, and emitted the immortal line; "Did ye change the wallpaper or something?"

Wallpaper patterns ranged all the way from typically traditional floral designs right up to some which bordered on the abstract. There was something a little bit fascinating about the repetitive nature of those patterns. I loved to watch Dad getting the sheets to match up. As I became older, I was sometimes entrusted with the job of painting the adhesive to the back of the paper. But, when it came to measuring, cutting and hanging the paper, only Dad did that; it was far too important a function to be entrusted to a mere junior like me; too much could go wrong, I suppose. Even when the entire kitchen was finally covered in the new wallpaper, there was still more to do; namely, the border. This was like a thin strip of wallpaper, no more than a couple of inches in width. Two strips ran all the way around the room, one along the bottom edge of the wallpaper, and another along the top. And though the pattern and the colours might be quite different from the main wallpaper, it had to somehow 'match'. I never understood how this judgment was made.

At one stage in the mid-sixties, some genius in the wonderful world of wallpaper design came up with the concept of a wallpaper pattern that was intended to reproduce the appearance of a dry-stone wall. Despite what many may believe to the contrary, design in the sixties did not always necessarily deliver long-term benefits to society. Sure there was the Mini car, and indeed the mini dress, and psychedelic album covers and so on. But there were also some tragedies, such as Hawkins House in Dublin, Nana Mouskouri's spectacles and even worse than those, wallpaper that was intended to resemble a stone wall. Why would anybody want such a thing in their home, particularly when one considers where we lived, already surrounded by literally hundreds of miles of stone walls? It was unconscionable, but that did not stop many people from decorating, or should I say desecrating their homes in this manner. To my shame, I have to admit that we did it ourselves, even to the point of following one of the other great misguided fashion statements of the time, namely putting the 'stony' wallpaper on just one wall of four. Typically that would be the wall that housed the fireplace/chimneybreast, whilst leaving the other walls covered in the usual bland flowery patterns. In other words, we had the worst of both worlds.

Getting the wallpaper to look good right up to and behind the kitchen dresser was an important part of the procedure. The dresser, a mighty piece of furniture, had to be pulled a foot or two away from the wall, allowing Dad to get the paper in behind it. Of course, he did not waste paper covering the entire area hidden by the dresser. No, that would be pointless, but it had to go in a few inches all the way around, thus giving the casual observer the impression that every inch of the wall was covered in the stuff. When the dresser was pulled out, a bit of a mad scramble ensued amongst us to be the first to find the lost pennies and other coins that had inevitably rolled in there during the year. Being small was a distinct advantage in that particular situation. I was a fearful little fellow though, and, more than once, the frightful idea entered my mind that I might be overlooked when the dresser was pushed back again, right against the wall. I imagined my poor crushed body would not be discovered until the following December. So, I did not spend too much time in there.

There is simply no way to describe the excitement of an evening like this; the entire kitchen, the room where a family grew up, was transformed in just a few hours, right before our eyes. When it was all done, with the huge dresser restored once more to its rightful position, you could stand back and gaze in awe at our Dad's handiwork. He was one of those people who could do more or less anything. And because he was so, I suppose we took it all for granted; I cannot recall a single occasion when any one of us turned to him after a session of decorating and said "Well done, Dad, that's a great job". I wish that I had done so.

The story of the origin of our kitchen dresser is a legend in itself. My grandparents had the house built in the 1920's. The dresser was ordered at that time, from a family business near Gort, a family whose speciality was furniture-making. The family in question was also involved in republican activities during the War of Independence. For this reason the house was raided by the British military authorities. Unable to find the individuals they sought, they satisfied their hunger for violence by burning the place down. And on the premises was the partly-finished dresser intended for our house. And, so, the dresser in our house to this day, is actually the Mark II version, the original having been destroyed in the fire.

As I said, Dad could do most things, including re-decorating, but having said that, it just recently occurred to me that I never actually saw him painting. Having said that, I do know that he once repainted an entire car, and did so by hand. The outcome was predictable, with brushstrokes visible everywhere; not one of his success stories. One of the peculiar things about our kitchen's interior walls was that there was a sort of divide about a metre up from the floor all the way around. This was like where a dado rail might exist, if we'd known about such a thing. Wallpaper was applied from the dividing-line upwards to the ceiling. Below the dividing-line, the walls were always painted. Why the divide? I don't know but I can only assume that it was the fashion at some time in the past. It had to be painted every year, and on one particular occasion my mother showed me how it was done. Naively, I feigned enthusiasm, as one was clearly intended to. I did not realise at the time that if you were once assigned a job, and proved to be reasonably effective at its accomplishment, well then you were stuck with it for all time. Every year, a new large can of paint was acquired, and an announcement went forth; "Johnny will paint the kitchen tonight". If I'd been clever and fore-sighted on that first occasion, I could have malingered with a "pain in my stomach" or some one of the usual complaints, thus avoiding the job forever. In fairness, it was not a very onerous task, and, besides, I did learn how to paint. Strangely, I can still remember the usual brand name on the paint cans; it was UNO. I don't know what became of UNO paint, but one never sees it now.

"The Christmas Box" - that was another task for our Dad on Christmas Eve or certainly on a day very shortly prior to Christmas Day. He would drive to the two or three nearby shops that we regularly supported throughout the year and purchase a number of items, mostly just regular groceries that were needed, with maybe a few more luxury-type things, suitable for the season. It was customary at Christmas for the shopkeeper to throw in one free item, which might be just a packet of tea or whatever. As soon as Dad got back home, my mother would inspect the "Christmas Box", i.e. the free item, and pass judgment accordingly. If it met with her approval she would say something like "Well, now, that was generous". However, if it was her opinion that the value of the extra item did not match up to her expectations, especially considering the money we had left in that shop during the previous twelve months, she would let fly; "That oul' miser, is that all she gave you?" What most strikes me now is how modest our requirements were.

The entire collection of goods from each shop fitted in what looked at the time like an enormous cardboard box. I can picture it now in my Dad's hands as he walked into the kitchen, and I realise that, in fact, it was actually quite a small cardboard box. The contents of a typical family's weekly outing to the supermarket today would probably equal ten such cardboard boxes. Obesity was not then an issue anyone had ever heard of. And as for the relatively small number of "luxury" items, these were usually no more than a tin of biscuits or even just a Swiss roll. In any case, for us it was another significant and exciting event in the build-up to the big day.

My mother kept some hens, turkeys, ducks and geese. Many of these birds were destined to meet their doom as the Christmas markets approached. Turkeys, hens and ducks lived out their relatively short lives in a large yard to the rear of the farmhouse. The geese, however, enjoyed a life of comparative liberty. When the flocks of young goslings had developed enough to follow their parents, not just walking but swimming, which comes naturally to them, the geese were left to their own devices, living on the river that meandered through our farm. Naturally, there is no obvious divide or border on a river to indicate where one farmer's territory ends and the next begins, yet the geese largely restricted themselves to the stretch of river that lay within our boundaries. How could a goose know a thing like that? And, since we're on the topic, why do people use that expression "silly goose"? It seems to me that geese are no sillier than any other bird; indeed if anything they may well be just that bit smarter. Respect is due to any domesticated species that can live amongst nature for months at a time, whilst simultaneously protecting its flock from various wild animals of prey. And if you attempt to approach too closely while goose-eggs are being hatched in the springtime, an extremely aggressive gander will certainly chase you away. As children, we knew well enough not to go near them at a time like that.

And what does any of this have to do with Christmas, you may well ask? Let me tell you. The geese fed themselves on the river for the bulk of the year, but about a month or so prior to their date with destiny, they needed to be rounded up and brought back close to the farmyard, so that they could be "fattened up". Again, I had been assigned this function once, and, thus, it was to be forever mine. Rounding up a flock of geese, especially one that has lived a totally undomesticated existence for many months of the year may be compared to marshalling mice at the crossroads. How do you persuade geese to abandon the river that has become their natural home? Even assuming you can get them to adapt to the life of the landlubber, how do you then point them in the general direction of the farmyard? How do you get them through gates and gaps in walls? How do you get them into a shed or outhouse? With great difficulty is the smart answer, even if it is the correct one. I might have got them three quarters of the way home, when they would suddenly change direction and head back towards the river, or worse still, split up into separate groups. It was an extremely frustrating task, and one I generally gave myself the guts of an entire day to accomplish.

On one such occasion, I witnessed an event which was certainly unique in my experience. After many hours, I had got finally got the flock of geese into a large field close to home. Suddenly, one goose made a bold dash for freedom, firstly running down a slight slope, quite fast for a goose, and then, to my utter astonishment, rising like a 747 to as much as a couple of feet above the ground. The flyaway goose maintained altitude for a couple of hundred yards before running out of field and returning to terra firma. I had never seen a domestic goose fly before, and did not realise they had the ability to do so. I never saw it again.

A number of specially-selected "fattened" specimens from amongst the collection of geese and turkeys would be taken to the market in Ennis to be sold. This was an all-day event and one that I never attended, so I cannot be expected to describe it. I do remember my parents arriving home after the day in town, exhausted and frozen from the effect of standing in an open marketplace all day long. Of course, it cannot have been thus, but it always appeared to be the case that the market was only allowed to be held on a day that was cold, wet and truly miserable. To add insult to injury, my mother always insisted that the prices eventually settled on between her and the various buyers were much less than what her exceptionally-reared birds deserved. She would declare that after all her hard work, including hand-feeding the geese and turkeys in their final weeks, the monetary reward did not match up to her expectations, and, so, she was very unlikely to rear birds for sale ever again. But just a couple of months later, she would once more be back preparing for the following year's crop of turkeys and geese.

Despite the presence of quite a selection of various types of fowl in our back yard right throughout the year, I do not recall that we ever had a visit from a fox. It's not that there were no foxes about. There certainly were and plenty of them, but they were very wild animals, totally unused to any contact with humans, other than when they were being hunted by packs of beagles, or targeted by hunters with shotguns. I suppose they had learned to be extremely wary of human contact, and thus were very unlikely to risk approaching anywhere close to a farmyard. In fact, it was very rarely that one would even observe a fox, and then only very much in the distance. The contrast could hardly be greater with the astonishingly common sightings of foxes in our cities today, casually wandering the streets, and brazenly using front and back gardens for their modern foraging grounds. I believe there is something quite pitiful about the sight of these once rather noble animals as they scavenge their way around our urban environment, reduced to a way of life no better than that of seagulls of magpies. The decent thing to do would be to get them out of our towns and cities for good and back to where they belong. How is this to be done? I'm sure I don't know.

Our Christmas tree was always a holly tree. Many people treat this revelation with incredulity, but in rural Ireland of more than half a century ago, this was commonplace. Artificial trees were out of the question. And it's not that there were no "traditional" Christmas trees available on our land. There were, and quite a number of them as it happened, because our Dad was in the habit of planting exactly such trees. However, no-one would dream of "wasting" these evergreens on a function as unimportant as brightening up a room for a few weeks at Christmas. The evergreen trees were grown especially in order to produce timber that would provide rafters for farm building projects and so on. Besides, holly bushes grew on local crags in profusion. Going out to cut down one of these was another seasonal function that I performed once and then followed through for every subsequent Christmas while I lived at home. Unlike rounding up geese, this was a job that I really enjoyed. I felt there was something very manly about setting out through the crags to select a suitable holly bush. All you needed was a saw and the patience to search until you found the right tree, one with the requisite quantity of the reddest berries imaginable. Sure, holly bushes are prickly but there is no better Christmas tree.

The division of labour between the sexes was even more extreme on Christmas Day than perhaps at any other time. My older brother Francis has always been into fishing and shooting for game. On Christmas Day, it was his habit to take the shotgun and go for a very long walk through the local countryside in search of duck, pheasant or whatever unfortunate bird crossed his path. I was never any use at any of these things. Nevertheless, once I was old enough to do so,

I often accompanied him on these Christmas morning missions. I don't remember that we ever actually brought down a single bird but the outing occupied a number of hours of the morning, bringing us nicely up to dinner time. We would arrive back from our labours in the wilderness, empty-handed, but ravenous with hunger and fully ready to get stuck into the turkey, the Christmas cake, the Christmas pudding and all the other usual trimmings. All morning long, while Francis and I had been strolling through the countryside like the gentry of old, my mother and my sisters worked really hard in a boiling hot kitchen to get everything ready for the big meal of the day, or of the year, really. I never seemed to notice what a raw deal the female occupants of the house endured at Christmas. That was just the way it was, and who were we to question it?

The rich food, which I loved, typically persisted for a few days, and then the remnants of turkey, Christmas cake and so on gradually diminished. During this period, I often overheard my mother say to acquaintances, "Oh, you'd get a bit sick of all that fancy food, wouldn't you? Sometimes you would just long for a plain slice of homemade bread and butter with a cup of tea". And her counterpart would inevitably concur, creating a general consensus that Christmas food was far too good for us, and the eventual return to our simple customary fare was something to be warmly welcomed. I completely failed to understand any of this. What were they talking about? I craved Christmas food and I never really had much time for traditional home-made bread. Who in their right mind would choose to consume plain brown bread, when rich fruit cake with decorative icing on top, as well as down the sides, was to be had? I would have happily consumed Christmas fare every day of the year, if only it were available. Really, adults were so out of touch.

As for Christmas desserts, of course plum pudding was king, but jelly and custard were not far behind. My favourite of all, though, was trifle – and it still is. On one unforgettable occasion, a couple of days after Christmas, a neighbour named Sean Glynn called to our house. He was offered tea, of course, that goes without saying, but, also, because of the season that was in it, and because there was still plenty of Christmas food in the house, my mother thought it would be courtesy to offer him a bowl of trifle. For some reason that she could not subsequently explain, the words she actually said to him were; "Sean, would you like a bowl of pig's mess?" He quickly declined, made his excuses and soon left. I do not remember him ever calling back.

For me, Christmas morning was the high point of the entire year. Since no words of mine would be adequate to describe the level of excitement and sheer joy that flowed from that event, I shall not attempt to do so. Suffice to say that Santa Claus performed spectacularly every time. As usual, the Catholic Church did its best to ruin all the fun. In our part of the world, this was achieved by having Christmas Day Mass at 7 o'clock in the morning. Yes, you read that right, 7AM. So, this is how things went. We got up at 6AM, discovered what Santa had laid on for us, played with the toys for a few minutes, and then got bundled into the car to travel to the parish church for Mass. No breakfast, notice. Mass was guaranteed to always be intensely boring, and Christmas morning Mass was no more or less so than any other day. But, just try to imagine the frustration of thinking about the fabulous trove of new toys lying uselessly at home while the priest droned endlessly on. He may have been praying for us, but we certainly were not praying for him. Why did normal human activity have to be suspended in favour of an event based on superstition and blind faith? Well, that is just the way it was. At last, we got home again and the day began properly. The first item on the agenda for our parents was a large fry-up for breakfast, in which we all joined as best we could without getting drawn away too much from the gifts that could now be enjoyed without further interruption.

There were some toys that were more or less guaranteed every year. For instance, almost always, each of us would receive a Christmas stocking that contained the occasional fun object, but was filled mostly with fairly useless stuff, forgotten in a few days. By contrast and in terms of something that could be treasured for years to come, there was nearly always a book as well. The 'Beano' or Dandy' annual, for example, with its hard shiny cover and with such a variety of excellent content inside; now there was a real treat. Toys that were driven by a simple clockwork mechanism were brilliant. There was an unfortunate trend towards replacing clockwork with battery-driven power in the early sixties. This was really frustrating as battery technology at the time was not very good so they tended to not last for very long; also batteries were quite expensive, and, worst of all, they were not rechargeable. One of the battery-powered toys I had was a small slide projector. A number of slide strips came with it, with just a few pictures on each strip, relating a very simple story. The projector worked alright but, naturally, we had seen all there was to see in just a few minutes. So, I made my own slide strips, drawing cartoons by hand on to transparent tissue paper. However, as I explained earlier I was not very good at drawing, so, despite my best efforts, the results were underwhelming, to say the least. Well, I did my best. I don't like to say it now, but when all is said and done guns were probably my favourite toy. I don't mean real guns, of course; no civilised society would allow such a thing in the hands of a child. These were just 'cap' guns, but we had endless hours of fun with them. I even had one that was complete with a holster that you could strap on to your thigh, just like a 'real' cowboy, so you could practice the 'fast draw'. I soon discovered that you could explode an entire roll of caps in just one go, by carefully placing it on a hard surface and swiftly banging down quite hard on it, with a large hammer. I would do this secretly, so that nobody was expecting it. It made a really mighty bang that reverberated all over the place. I always expected family members, or, if I were really lucky, maybe even neighbours, to come running, crying out, 'Oh God, what was that terrible noise, what happened at all?' To my great disappointment, there was never any reaction whatsoever.

Nothing lasts forever and, even as children, we knew that the time would come when growing up would have to be faced, and faced without benefit of the annual visit from Santa Claus. It's not something any child really wants to think about, and so, in general, we chose to do exactly that, i.e. we did not think about it. Hope springs eternal, or whatever. I was the second youngest, so naturally as the years rolled on, there were less and less of us still qualifying for Santa's deliveries. A Christmas morning finally arrived when I raced down the stairs as always and rushed into the kitchen to inspect everything on display. I immediately saw that there was just one set of gifts left there, and they were for my younger sister, Rose. Santa had forgotten me! I could not conceal the shock and my mother noticed the look on my face. "Oh sure, you're too old now for Santa", she said. She said it kindly, but it might have been kinder had it been said to me on any one of the 364 days since the previous Christmas. I proceeded to put on the socks and shoes that had been kept warm overnight by the range, whilst doing my best to hold back the flood of tears that I should have let flow. In the course of a lifetime, one must expect to encounter occasional disappointments. I have known few to match that one.

A good few years later, when I was a teenager, I awoke one Christmas morning to see the unmistakable outline of an LP in a paper bag. There was no mistaking those square thin bags; anyone who ever bought an LP knows what I mean. By this time I had begun to assemble a very small record collection, mostly Beatles and Rolling Stones. Rather than jump out and inspect it immediately, I lay in bed for some time building up the expectation. What could it be? Perhaps Simon and Garfunkel - after all, I had none of theirs. Then again, maybe it was Bob Dylan, or Jimi Hendrix. And who had bought the record? Finally, I could torture myself no longer and looked inside. Before I had even fully withdrawn the record from the bag, the miserable truth was evident: "Songs from My Fair Lady". Everyone knew I was into rock music. And I never liked musicals. Whose idea was it to leave it there where I would discover it first thing in the morning - and why? I never asked and I never found out.

The house filled up at Christmas as my older brothers and sisters returned from boarding school or, in later years, from the jobs they now held, away from home. There was simply not enough room for everybody in the bedrooms upstairs, so something had to give. I was assigned temporary sleeping quarters in a room downstairs; the "parlour" or what would now be called a sitting-room. For a bed, I used the sofa in the corner. This did not resemble a modern, luxurious couch. It was shaped like an antique chaise lounge. For all I know perhaps it was an antique chaise lounge. All I know is that it was quite small, barely wide enough to lie on. And because it was once assigned to me, then, of course, it was to be my bed-space for every subsequent Christmas. As the years passed, and I grew longer, my legs began to hang over the end, and so I had to append a stool there to cater for expansion. It sounds really uncomfortable now, but I never had the slightest difficulty about sleeping there. On the contrary, I felt somehow privileged, just because I was on my own, I think, in what seemed like a rather superior location. Also, I did not have to suffer listening to anybody snoring. And, furthermore, bats were not an issue downstairs. Yes, as would have been the case in many older country houses, we occasionally had these little animals (or are they birds?) around the place. At one stage a bat took up residence hanging on to the curtains at the landing window. At first, of course, he was an object of some fascination to us. He slept there all day, with his claws dug in to the fabric. If you gently poked or prodded at him, he would just sort of shrug a little bit, but carry on sleeping. Night time though, that was a different matter. If a bat got in your bedroom, he would endlessly fly up and down the length of the room, apparently seeking a way out. You would have to get up and open a door or window to get it out of the room. I remember having a bat in my room once, flying up and down like that in the middle of the night, and then suddenly going suspiciously quiet. I firstly thought that he had found his own way out and so I prepared to go back to sleep. But soon I could feel something crawling up along the bedclothes, getting closer and closer to my head. There used to be a myth going around to the effect that if a bat got entangled in your hair, then you just would not be able to get him out of it, or, at least, not without having your head shaved. I didn't really believe it, but, at the same time, one does not wish to take a chance in a situation like that. I got rid of him somehow. It's interesting what you can get used to. When I tell some people about this, you would think that I'd had a visitation from Count Dracula himself. It was just a little bat, that's all.

There were no very wealthy families in our neighbourhood. Most of us grew up on small farm holdings and enjoyed what, to us, seemed a reasonable standard of living, if, indeed, we ever stopped to think about such a thing. I have little doubt that by today's very different standards, some families would be defined as having lived "below the poverty line". There was one family nearby that did live a life of poverty and quite severe deprivation. Unfortunately for the children in this family, parenting skills were notably absent in both father and mother. During one Christmas holiday period, we had a visit from some of these kids. Roughly the same ages as we were, they also attended the same local school. On some previous very cold winter holiday seasons, they had been in the habit of calling to join us and to spend a day "skating" on the ice that formed on the pond near our home. On this particular year, there was no ice to entice them over. They were driven by hunger. My mother recognised their desperate situation, and quickly organised food for them. She invited them to sit at the kitchen table to eat, but they evidently could not even bring themselves to take the time to do so. They ate from their hands, standing up. Unfortunately, we are all aware that scenes like that are still repeated in many places around the world on a daily basis. To this day, I can identify the spot on our kitchen floor where I stood transfixed and watched with a peculiar mixture of shame and fascination as our school colleagues and playmates ravenously consumed as much food as they could, as quickly as they could.

The ice-skating I referred to above was something we accomplished wearing whatever boots, shoes or wellingtons we happened to have on our feet on any given day. None of us had ever seen a pair of ice skates in our lives. What we did have was a lot of fun. The pond was only a few yards wide and about twice as long, I suppose, but, to us, it could have been the canals of Amsterdam. It usually took a few frosty nights before the ice was solid enough to support our weight. There was always the fear that the cold spell would end before the ice hardened sufficiently. A really good year was one where the icy weather lasted for a full week or even longer – the kind of winter that grown-ups would be whingeing about, while we enjoyed every moment of it, never feeling the cold at all. There was one grown-up who did enter into the spirit of it all, though, and that was our Dad, who liked to frighten the life out us by jumping up and down on the ice as hard as he could right in the middle of the pond. The entire surface would emit a loud splitting sound, and you could actually see the cracks spread out from him reaching all over the ice. I feared he would drown if he fell through; he never did fall through. I understand now that the water beneath the ice was no more than a couple of feet deep anyway.

Speaking of water and the danger associated with it, there was so much of it around, we could all have drowned ten times over, and it is amazing that we did not. In between the patches of good land, we were surrounded by ponds, lakes, drains, bog-holes, wells, streams and a river. Not one of us could swim properly. Sometimes, I break into a cold sweat just thinking how close to death we must have been on so many occasions. However, the only person I ever witnessed actually falling in the water was a neighbouring boy who called over from time to time for the usual games of football and so on. One wintry day, he and I went for a walk in the rough territory near our home. There had been a good deal of rain and the water was high. As we crossed over a flooded stream, hopping from rock to rock in the nimble way that only youngsters can, he mistook a floating piece of wood for a rock. Down he went, right up to his neck. With my help, he managed to scramble out. It was a freezing cold day with a biting wind and he was, of course, almost entirely soaked apart from his head and one arm. We made our way back towards my house, but to my amazement, he refused to come in and dry out. I suspect he knew my mother would insist that he change into dry clothes (probably mine), and he just did not want to go there. He proved his hardiness by hopping on his bicycle and heading off to cycle the distance of a mile or so to his home. Naturally, my mother predicted that he would die of pneumonia. Happily, I can report that he is alive and well, almost sixty years later.

One particularly severe winter, not only was everything frozen over, but that was then followed by a heavy fall of snow. Falls of snow like that were not usually a feature of winters in the west of Ireland, and so on the rare occasion when it did happen, we really made the most of it, building snowmen and throwing snowballs. As well as the frozen pond near our home, there was also a series of lakes just a few hundred yards away. Lake water did not usually freeze unless the cold weather was really severe. That winter it was very severe and the lakes did freeze over. One evening, my brother Francis and I set out to walk right across, not just one lake, but two of them in succession. I can still just about remember the fascination of watching the trail of broken snow as I unquestioningly followed in my older brother's footsteps And then we walked all the way back across the two lakes again, arriving home in darkness. It was only when we explained where we had been that we were made to realise what a dangerous mission we had set out on. Lake ice can be treacherous, being much thinner in some parts of a lake than in others. Had we fallen through the ice, nobody would have been any the wiser what became of us until it was all much too late. I am not a religious person, but I sometimes wonder what kind of spirit of the lakes kept us from wandering into the danger zone on that evening of chilly adventure. Or maybe we were just lucky.

We invested a certain amount of effort into various other schemes to accumulate riches. One of these was to participate in the St. Stephens Day practice of Wren Boys, the day after Christmas Day. The idea was to conceal one's identity, usually wearing some form of mask, and then go from house to house in the neighbourhood, singing or playing music or dancing or whatever. Musical skill was not really necessary, but it would have helped. Our masks were primitive and so the neighbours invariably guessed one's identity. This was to our advantage, as they were more likely to be generous to someone they knew. They also knew that to turn away a neighbour's child would not go down well with the parents of that child. When I was old enough to be a Wren Boy, perhaps about ten years old or so, I took to the road, expecting to be rich by nightfall. I had taken a few lessons in how to play a very limited number of traditional Irish tunes on the tin whistle – very badly. My companion, a school colleague, had even less musical skill than I - in other words he had none at all, and so he simply beat time on the ground using a piece of a stick. Actually, he could not really beat time either, but at least he gave it a good effort. The Everly Brothers had nothing to worry about. When we split the proceeds at the end of the day, it was clear that we had not found the short cut to financial independence. The following year, I decided to take to the road on my own. That turned out to be an error of judgment. Having walked miles and accumulated just a few shillings, I was set upon by a rival pair of Wren Boys. The only things I can say in their favour is that, number one, they did not actually beat me up, and number two, for some inexplicable reason, they did not take quite all my money from me, just most of it. Naturally, they wore masks, and so could not be identified. To this day, I do not know who those two boys were. Even so, I hate them both with a deep abiding hatred that has not lessened with the passage of time.

School

The primary school that we attended was called Moyrhee National School. It was a small one-teacher school that had been established back in the 1860's, and was named after the locality. It was located right in the heart of the countryside in a very remote place, several miles from even the nearest small village in either direction. When I first went there as a five-year-old, there were thirty pupils in all. By the time I left, in 1965, there were just thirteen. It finally closed not very long afterward, as practically all such tiny schools were shut down for good in the mid-sixties. As you can see, the name, Moyrhee, is not very easy to spell correctly. It's easy to get it wrong, and I'm not quite certain that I have it right even now. Here's a puzzle for you; what other word can you think of that features the letters 'y', 'r' and 'h' in that order? And that's assuming I have it right. The closest I can think of is "myrrh" – but that has two r's between the y and the h. On one rather stressful occasion, the teacher found that I was unable to spell the word correctly. "The name of your own school!" she practically screamed at me. "It's even written on the wall outside the front door" she added, piling on the humiliation. And, indeed it was, but why would anybody ever look at that? It may still be written there for all I know or care.

We were told that the name Moyrhee was an anglicised version of the original Irish name, and, indeed, this is the case with many place-names in Ireland. I shall not even attempt to spell the Irish version, since, as you now know, I have trouble enough with it in English. The theory was that it meant "the plain of the kings". I have a problem with that. Considering the very hilly and undulating nature of all the surrounding territory, it would take a fleet of at least a hundred excavators and bulldozers working for a year just to construct a small runway, never mind an entire plain. And as for the kings, well, the kings of spades, clubs, hearts and diamonds were the only ones we were familiar with.

I can barely recall my first days at school. Because it was a single-teacher school, the teacher was in the habit of delegating the business of looking after the new and very young pupils, such as me, to some of the older girls from fifth or sixth class – never boys, for whatever reason. These 'big' girls were, to me anyway, indistinguishable from the 'real' teacher, leading to a considerable degree of confusion.

We were driven by fear; fear of the teacher, and by extension, fear of failure. The sheer pressure led me to experience some type of 'brain-fade' on at least one occasion. This must have been a couple of years in, as we were by now reading very simple short poems and we were expected to commit them to memory. Having evidently failed at this task, a group of us were put standing to one side and told to learn the poem in question. I tried hard, reading it over and over to myself, until I was convinced that I had it nailed. I must have overdone it, because, quite suddenly I found that the words I had previously recognised and understood, suddenly made no sense whatsoever. Incredibly, there was not a single word that I knew on the page. Where had they gone? I began to panic, realizing that I was now certain to fail the upcoming test from the teacher. What was I to do? And then, just as suddenly, I found what was wrong. I had temporarily neglected to read the words from left to right across the page, mistakenly doing the exact opposite. You should try it sometime. That's a lot more than sixty years ago, but I still remember the first line of the poem in question. It was 'Fly, fly away', so what I had - temporarily - tried to learn was 'yawa ,ylf ,ylF'. I never made that mistake again.

Moyrhee School photo: John Brew, front row, second from left.
Gerita, second row, fifth from left. Francis, back row, second from left.

Every morning, before classes began, and every evening, when they ended, the classroom floor had to be swept clean. That was a job for us, the pupils. The first two to arrive in the morning were expected to attend to it. How the pair was chosen for each evening is something I have forgotten. I could understand how the floor would need sweeping after a day's classes had been completed. But how did the dust accumulate while the space was unoccupied overnight? And dust there always was – it was a mystery to me. I didn't mind being early and having to sweep the floor because it meant I could spend some time listening to the music from the teacher's radio, music which carried in from her quarters in the adjoining room. I actually recall hearing songs by Cliff Richard, and even more specifically, Dominic Behan singing 'Liverpool Lou'.

The teacher was a temperamental individual. Also, she was not a very good teacher. In later life, whenever I thought about it, I've always been amazed at how much knowledge we did actually gain in school, despite her worst efforts. For example, by the age of ten or eleven, we had somehow managed to grasp the concept of compound interest, not the simplest of topics for a child to get their head around. But much more difficult than that was the fundamental structure of the currency in use at the time. This was based on the pound, and there was then no distinction between the Irish pound and the pound sterling. The breakdown of the pound was intricate and complex. There were twenty shillings to the pound, and each shilling was divided into twelve pennies. Of course, there was no suggestion of decimalisation anywhere; that would have been far too simple for a so-called "Imperial" system. Each penny could be further broken down into two half-pennies. These half-pennies were of little value, but were still in circulation. Incredibly, each penny could also be described as being divided into four farthings. Now, a farthing would have been of such little value that nobody would want to carry such a useless thing around with them. Luckily, they no longer existed in real life, and I'm not sure that I can recall ever holding one in my hand. The really amazing thing about it, though, was that our maths textbooks featured farthings all over the place, as though they were still in daily use, which they had not been for many years, or maybe decades, for all we knew. This meant that the basic unit of currency, the pound, not worth much more than today's euro, could be described as being equivalent to almost a thousand constituent pieces, actually 960 farthings, to be exact. The purchasing power of one mythical farthing would probably equate to no more than a few grains of sugar. We were expected to become expert in calculations based on pounds, shilling and pence, as well as half-pennies. And farthings, including, the notional concept of "three farthings". Somehow, we did it - I really don't know how. Imagine trying to work out how many items at two pounds, fourteen shillings and seven pence, plus three farthings could be purchased from a total sum of thirty-seven pounds, seventeen shillings and three pence. (I make that out to be fourteen items, by the way, with a tiny amount of change left over). We were just kids and yet we practically had to be mathematical geniuses.

Much later in life I found it interesting to realise that whilst we were learning about the geography of, not only our own country, but that of Britain as well, our contemporaries in school over there were being taught almost nothing about either the history or geography of Ireland, their next door neighbours. And then our Irish history book was structured in a very peculiar manner. There was a deal of space devoted to characters such as Fionn mac Cumhail, Cuchulainn and the Fir Bolg; of course, these were not actually historical figures at all, but rather fictional characters that only existed in myths and legends. On the other hand, our history of Ireland stopped dead at the 1916 rising. We left primary school having been taught nothing whatsoever about some of the most significant periods in the history of our own nation, namely the War of Independence and the Civil War. It would seem that even thirty to forty years on, in the 1950's and 1960's, these events were too recent and therefore too divisive to even get mentioned. It was simpler to let on that they had never happened.

The teacher was not unusual in her time. Ineffectual, bad-tempered teachers were the order of the day in the Irish primary education system. Ours was by no means the worst. We sometimes heard reports of teachers in other schools in the general area who were utter savages. Some were even taken to court for excessive cruelty to children, though legal measures of that sort were rare. Our teacher, Mrs. Callinan, occasionally let slip very rare moments of humour or even generosity – not often, mind you. I believe that she actually had something of a soft spot for me. On the odd occasion when freebies were to be handed out, I was often the favoured one. I don't know why. By freebies I mean posters, or booklets that would have been distributed to schools for educational purposes. One that I can remember was an Aer Lingus handout; a rather lavish full-colour promotional publication that contained information about not just the airline itself, but also the very nature of manned fight. It was the first time I came across the concepts of thrust, lift, weight and drag – which I never forgot. Right away, I determined that I was going to become an Aer Lingus pilot. By the time I was a teenager, I had moved on, adamant that I could not serve in any capacity that required the wearing of a uniform. I just wanted to be a hippie. Subsequently, I took up a career in the merchant marine as a ship's Radio Officer, a job that required, yes, you guessed it, the wearing of a uniform. After all, one is entitled to change one's mind from time to time. Anyway, the teacher's largesse with these handouts wasn't working - the fact remained I disliked her as much as all the other pupils did. I was also relatively lucky in that I was, I suppose, a student of at least average ability, or perhaps better that that; it's not for me to judge. I was able to learn most things and to be prepared, thus pre-empting and avoiding the worst excesses of the teacher's mad bursts of temper. But we had classmates who, in today's more enlightened world, would certainly fall within the category of children with learning difficulties. There was no recognition then of conditions such as dyslexia, and so, of course, there was no diagnosis of it. Any pupil who could not keep up was labelled as "stupid". The teacher had her own peculiar vocabulary too. For instance, she appeared to have some kind of morbid fascination with the legal system, referring to people's court appearances as being 'on the green table' and prison sentences as time spent 'behind Shaws'. Shaws was a department store in

Limerick, which apparently was in the vicinity of the prison. If a pupil's attendance record at school was erratic in nature, she would declare that 'you cannot come and go as you please, you know; after all, this is not a hotel'. Not one of us had ever even been inside the door of a hotel. Nevertheless we were certainly well aware that time spent in such an establishment would likely be a very different experience compared to what we were undergoing. Each time she repeated this mantra, I became a little more fascinated with the concept of being able to 'come and go as you please' and could not wait for a real taste of it. To this day, when I stay in any hotel, the phrase invariably comes to mind. I like hotels, perhaps for that very reason. If you dared speak back to the teacher, the phrase she favoured was "the impertinence of you". I considered this to be comically close to "the *importance* of you". Also, when she chose to ridicule our feeble attempts to solve a mathematical problem, she would declare "that's just mental", presumably meaning to indicate that one should not even need to use pen and paper in order to perform such a simple calculation. She seemed entirely unaware that defining an activity as "mental" meant something quite different to us. Of course, Irish words were mainly preferred for belittling us, and typical of these would be "amadan" and "oinseach". The online Irish-English translation services reveal these to be equivalent to "idiot" and "fool". It seemed there was no limit in terms of the various names that the teacher was prepared to use when it came to belittling us. Occasionally, in a fit of extreme bad temper she would call one of us a 'reptile'. I found that there was something fascinating, and also a little bit disgusting about this. Why the word 'reptile'? When one thinks of reptiles, one immediately thinks of snakes, and in Ireland, snakes were regarded as the lowest form of life, apparently having been vanquished from the country by our great saviour, St. Patrick. This type of nonsense was taken quite seriously in those times. I can still picture her, all red-faced and quivering with rage, as she spat out the words, "You reptile, you!" Today, I suppose a teacher could be dismissed from service for unfavourably comparing a child to a cold-blooded life-form, slithering and venomous. We had no such protection, having to take whatever was dished out to us. Did it make us stronger or weaker? I wonder.

Why were many teachers so bad at teaching and at cherishing the children in their care? I have no idea. Perhaps somebody has done research into the matter. Were they properly trained? Indeed, I wonder if they received any training at all. If they did, it must have been brief and rudimentary and they were certainly not over-burdened with any degree of expertise in the field of child psychology. One can appreciate that for one teacher to maintain control of an entire school required a degree of discipline. It may well be the case that it was an extremely frustrating experience for the teacher, day in and day out. And it's not as if any of us were ever likely to say thanks to her on the way out the door after a day at school. But why did they take it out on us, helpless children?

As an example of the hopeless nature of Mrs. Callinan's teaching methods, take the day she told my class that we were about to learn how to do Long Division. In case you have forgotten, or you knew it by some other name, Long Division was the process whereby a fairly large number is divided by another fairly large number – definitely not "mental". The experience is seared in my memory – for all the wrong reasons. She rarely used the blackboard, but she took to it for this particular lesson. Long Division is like anything else you learn in life, ranging from simple tasks such as picking up a toy and playing with it, all the way up to advanced astrophysics – it can be quite straightforward when you know how to do it, but rather difficult when you do not. And so, it has to be carefully explained the first time around. I had never heard of Long Division prior to this, and had no idea what she was talking about. Her initial approach would ideally have included a short introductory talk about what Long Division actually was and why it might be beneficial to know something about it. She skipped that part. Her method was as simple as it was useless. She herself executed one example of Long Division on the blackboard. Then she asked each of us in turn to repeat the exercise. What she had done on the board may as well have been in Roman numerals for all it meant to me – I understood nothing. She raged and fumed at our inability to grasp the fundamentals of this basic mathematical exercise, which she clearly felt had been adequately demonstrated. Within a few minutes, our allotted time-span was exhausted; she had other classes to look after. As far as she was concerned, our class had been taught the essence of how to perform Long Division. Of course, I subsequently did learn how it was done; possibly from my older siblings or from my parents, I cannot remember, but certainly not from the so-called teacher. Her work was entirely in vain.

In my earliest years at school, I was a little behind in learning to read, and the so-called educational system certainly did not help at all. I learned more from my parents and my sisters and brothers than I ever learned from the teacher. I recall that the documents I found most useful to gain experience in reading from were comics, such as the Beano and the Dandy. That's where I obtained and expanded my vocabulary. In later years, I moved on to books and newspapers, but I never lost the love for illustrated publications. In the 50's and 60's a brilliant series called 'Classics Illustrated' was published. As the name suggests these were great works of literature converted to comic-book style. Naturally, the stories had to be somewhat compressed to fit the comic-book format, but the essential content was retained, and the illustrations were of the highest standard. I loved them. I particularly remember being firstly acquainted with well-known works such as 'The War of the Worlds',

'Moby Dick', and 'A Tale of Two Cities'. I have not seen any of these since I was a child but, to this day, I can still visualise some of the striking illustrations contained in them. I'm not sure if it is a good or a bad thing to be able to claim that you can bluff your way through life to a certain extent by giving the impression that you have actually read the full version of these books. For instance, although I have not yet read the real thing, I know which book contains the line, 'It is a far, far better thing that I do, than I have ever done'. Do you? Ok, I admit it, I am being a smartass. In my early teenage years I moved on to 'super-hero' comics, featuring 'The Incredible Hulk', 'Batman', 'Spiderman' and so on. A classmate and I swapped these all the time. I built up a large collection over time and they would possibly be of some value now, if I still had them. Of course, they were all long since consigned to the dustbin.

In his time, our Dad had attended the same school as we did; and probably our grandfather as well. In the 1920's, a century ago now, when Dad was there, the standard of teaching was even worse. He rarely spoke of his time there, but I recall him once telling us about an experience with his teacher, Mrs. Fitzgibbons. She was conducting a history lesson about the ancient High King of Ireland, Brian Boru, and how his forces were victorious against the Vikings at the Battle of Clontarf, but how Brian himself met his death there. The legend was that he knelt in his tent, praying for victory as his soldiers fought valiantly outside. A Viking called Bruadar came upon Brian in his tent and killed him. We all learned about that in our time too. But Mrs. Fitzgibbons added a dash of her own drama to the story. In her version, Bruadar burst into the tent, and "shot Brian Boru dead". Quite a feat, considering this was in 1014, and the invention of handguns was still hundreds of years away.

School life was so different from home life they might well have been two different worlds. At home you were expected to do some work, but you also had freedom and fun. At school, the driving factor was fear, and one soon learnt to give nothing away to the teacher. Anything you did say was liable to be used in evidence against you later on, so there was safety in a sullen silence. Moving from one environment to the other, we essentially assumed different personalities, exhibiting different behaviours. Perhaps we were a little bit like those who regularly crossed the border between East and West Germany or between North and South Korea. I believe that, over time, we developed a kind of protective shell for the world of school, thus suppressing normal childlike behaviour. This is very evident to me now when I recall what happened when a substitute teacher was temporarily appointed. This came about when, to our great joy, Mrs. Callinan became seriously ill and had to be hospitalised for a major operation. Naturally, we hoped that she would succumb to the surgeon's scalpel. The substitute teacher was a young woman, newly qualified, I believe. Teacher training must have come on a great deal because her general approach to educating children was entirely different to what we were used to. I think I was still only in infants or first class, I'm not sure, but anyway I was very young. To our amazement, this new teacher was kind and gentle with us. We were not accustomed to anything like that. Furthermore, instead of using dry and boring schoolbooks, she read us fairytales and nursery rhymes. But did not fairytales and nursery rhymes belong on the opposite side of the border, in the home? This was strange and unusual behaviour, entirely unexpected from a teacher. I suppose she was attempting to break down that border, the artificial divide between home life and school life. We had great difficulty processing this conflict, and sad to relate, I believe that the effort on her part was almost entirely unsuccessful. The protective shell we had created around ourselves was solid and unbreakable. We had programmed ourselves to be untrusting and suspicious of those in a position of authority outside the home. And so, we did not reciprocate, remaining sullen and unresponsive, just as we had prepared ourselves to be. When I think of it now, how the poor woman must have despaired of us. The even sadder part of the story is that, when the time came for her to depart, we did not greatly mourn her loss, since we had not allowed ourselves to warm to her personality in the first place. And even though we certainly did not welcome Mrs. Callinan back to work, following her full recovery, at least now we were once again dealing with a phenomenon that we knew and understood. The status quo had been restored. I don't know what became of our substitute teacher. I can only hope that she encountered some degree of success in getting through to more responsive children in other schools.

For very young children starting out in primary school, a system existed that has long since disappeared. It was customary to begin to attend school after the Easter break, thus completing just one term before the Summer holidays. Since the children who began school at this time were typically just about four years old or so, it was the one short period during which the teacher would tend to be not too hard on them, corporal punishment, for example, being completely out of the question. Once September came though, you qualified as a fully-fledged member of the student body, and from that point onward, the gloves were off as far as the teacher was concerned. One particular year, when a new pupil I shall call Dennis (not his real name) arrived after the Easter break, we all witnessed a dreadful departure from this convention. Dennis and his older sister started school the same day. Parents sometime thought it was a good idea to send two young kids to school together in order not to separate them, even though that meant either one was about a year too old, or else, the other was about a year too young. Dennis was about a year too young. He found his first day at school extremely stressful. He bawled and cried incessantly all morning long, and simply could not be consoled – not that there was a great deal in the way of consolation to be found in that austere environment anyway. By eleven o'clock or so, he was grasping the doorknob with both hands, hanging off it in a desperate attempt to escape from the classroom. Failing to get the door open, he resorted to more extreme methods, kicking the door with his heavy boots. Up until that point, the teacher had held her nerve, but now she cut loose, slapping poor Dennis into submission. For the rest of the day, he sat at his desk, crying his heart out. For the rest of us, who thought that we had seen it all, it was an unforgettable lesson. Nothing was sacred now; the unwritten rule had been broken – a small child could be beaten even on its very first day at school.

We lived in dread of the arrival of the School Inspector. He - and it was always a man - would put us through our paces with a series of questions, all of which we were expected to be able to answer to a good standard. The teacher regularly made it clear that the feared inspector could arrive at any time, with zero warning, and failure on our part to measure up would have serious consequences. But what were these "serious consequences" likely to be? We were never told that and, needless to say, it would have been near-suicidal to ask. Of course, the real truth, which we were never told, was that it was the teacher who was being inspected, not the pupils. Had we known that, we could have exposed her to utter ignominy, deliberately failing to answer the simplest question put to us by the inspector. I can recall an occasion when her poor level of spoken Irish was shown up, as she failed to understand a question that the inspector put to her. Humiliated, she was reduced to shamefacedly muttering a request to him, asking him to repeat his query through English. One of the tasks that the inspector might demand from any pupil was to relate a 'sceal' – that is, a story through Irish. Needless to say the teacher had primed us with a selection of ready-made sceals (scealai?) that we were all expected to have committed to memory. The most ridiculous of these, that I can recall, spelt out the story of a cat who found a tall hat and a gun. He went out and killed a bird, which he then ate, apparently, coming home satisfied. So far, so good, but the really tricky part came when the teacher would then ask you in Irish, first of all, if the cat ate the bones, and then if he ate the feathers. We always had several cats about the place at home, and I never once witnessed any of them consume either feathers or bones. But one of these was meant to be true, whilst the other was meant to be false. As far as I could tell, it was quite impossible to give the correct answer. It was a trap. If she asked you did the cat eat the bones and you replied 'Sea' (for 'yes'), she would cry out 'Ni Shea!' (for 'no'). However, if you had replied 'Ni Shea', she would triumphantly yell 'Sea!' And the same rigmarole applied to the question of the feathers. Quite simply, you could not win. Pretty soon, you gave up trying to get it right and just gave a random answer, since it made no difference anyway. The real lesson you had learned was that the dice was loaded in favour of the house.

There was also another type of inspector, one who specialised in religious knowledge, or to be more specific, the rules and regulations of the Catholic Church. Teaching the ins and outs of Catholic religion took precedence over everything else in school, as it did in various other spheres of Irish life. This alternative inspector was a priest, and was known as the Diocesan Inspector, or as my brother Francis privately renamed him, the "dyin' ass" inspector. Failure to satisfactorily respond to such an interrogation would be regarded as a serious matter, and so, the teacher felt it was incumbent upon her to invest a huge amount of time and effort into dragging us up to the expected standard. This campaign on her part could involve everything from pleading, exhortations, threats and bullying, all the way up to sustained verbal abuse, and, if necessary, beatings with a stick. So much went into preparing us for this vital examination that we almost became mini-theologians, no doubt at the expense of trivial subjects like history, geography, English and mathematics. Once, Francis excelled himself in this test, when the inspector asked him what Church he belonged to. He was expected to reply by saying "the Catholic Church". But Francis understood him to mean at what actual church did he regularly attend Mass, and so he confidently answered "Tubber", the location of our parish chapel. It was the perfect answer, really. I wish that I had thought of it.

Various prayers were recited throughout the day at regular intervals. These were led by the teacher and we were all expected to join in. As far as I could tell, everyone did – except me. I never could learn prayers. So I just mouthed along and mostly got away with it. Other tests were sterner, though, and this is where I ran into difficulties. For some reason that I still do not understand, not only were we expected to learn many prayers off by heart in English, but also, the very same prayers in Irish as well. I was never great at Irish either, so this created a perfect storm for me. There was one prayer that was particularly challenging to learn; the brief title appeared deceptively simple, yet also enigmatic - "En Ego". I guess that part was Latin; it's not like anybody ever explained anything. It was hard enough through English. Google it and see for yourself. Through Irish it was a hellish experience. The daddy of them all, though, was a thing called the "rosary". This was not just one prayer but an entire collection of them, like a "Top Thirty" of prayers or maybe even a "Hot 100", all strung together in an infuriatingly tedious series of soliloquies that seemed to go on forever. Incredibly, there were even different versions of it for different days of the week - I never figured out the key to that. The big danger with the rosary was that audience participation formed a significant part of its make-up i.e. you could be called upon to take an active part in the proceedings. And this was an issue for someone who could not even regurgitate the simplest of them all – the "Hail Mary".

The priests from the village of Ruan, about three miles away, were regular visitors to the school. The more senior man, the parish priest, was Father Gunning, and we paid no heed whatsoever to him, since he did not show the slightest interest in us either. That arrangement suited everybody. He and the teacher often spent a great deal of time talking to each other. What about, we did not know or care. All we knew was that this was essentially free time for us. The junior man, or curate, was a saintly chap called Father Leamy, who was always nice to us. But he became very ill, I believe it was cancer, and died. On his final visit to our school, shortly before passing away, he brought us a large box of sweets, something that we normally received only on the day of the summer holidays. Our teacher, Mrs. Callinan, had hero-worshipped him, and there were reports that, upon hearing the news of his demise, she was seen on her knees in the school yard, her arms raised to heaven, beseeching the recently departed curate to, "Take me up with you, Father, take me up!" The following day, we arrived to school at the usual time to be greeted by a closed door bearing a hand-written notice that read, "No school tomorrow". We were puzzled by this. Did "No school tomorrow" mean that there was actually school today, or not? Naturally, we assumed the preferred outcome, namely that the teacher, in her stupidity, had fixed the sign to the door the previous evening, apparently not realising that by the time we got to read it, it would by then, of course, actually be "tomorrow". We crept away silently in case we were seen by her. A day off! Even in death, Father Leamy was kind to us. On the way home, we memorialised his passing in an entirely irreverent manner, making up a little rhyme to fit the positive nature of the occasion; "No school tomorrow, said the fat vegetable marrow."

The new curate who replaced Father Leamy was an over-enthusiastic young priest called Father Carmody, and he was one seriously annoying individual. He was inclined to take the entire

Catholic religion thing far too much to heart for my liking. In the course of one of his first visits to our school he took it upon himself to display to us the various objects that would typically be used by a priest whilst administering the last rites to the dead, or to those who are deemed to be about to depart. These consisted of various small cylindrical containers that presumably contained oils or incense or whatever it is that is supposed to be deployed on such an occasion. Quite why he assumed that we would have the slightest interest in such a morbid topic, I do not know. In the event, he let the various pieces fall on to the floor, whereupon, they rolled in under our desks and other school furniture. A scramble ensued to retrieve the sacred objects. We were not quite sure whether we were even allowed to touch them. In any case, the promised demonstration quickly descended into a farcical display of epic incompetence. I trust he never had to deploy the afore-mentioned tackle for real. He usually called on a Friday afternoon, and on one such occasion, when I was by now one of the senior pupils in the school, he took it upon himself to test our ability to recite the usual Catholic prayers. He selected various pupils at random, most of them acquitting themselves perfectly. I was confident that my weak spot, my total inability to properly recite any prayers at all, would not be exposed; after all, I had got away with it for years at school. But my lucky streak was about to run out. He turned to me, setting me a task that would have been simple for most. Perhaps it was 'The Lord's Prayer' (or, as we called it, the "Our Father"), or one of those, I don't remember. Anyway, to his surprise, after stumbling my way along as best I could, I finally gave up about half way through. I assumed he would move on to the next victim after just one test; that was always how this sort of thing had gone up until then. But, no, he persisted with me, working his way through the entire litany of all the various prayers that we were expected to know off by heart. I could not successfully recite any one of them.

He was deeply shocked and completely furious with me. This was all bad enough, but at least he was not due to call again for a few weeks – perhaps he would forget all about the entire matter. Weren't priests supposed to have busy lives? The real problem person, as I saw it, was the teacher, who had silently witnessed the entire spectacle. I felt sure that, in her eyes, I had let down the school, and perhaps, in the process, exposed her sub-standard teaching methods. The whole process had dragged on for so long it was now time for us to go home, and thus I escaped her immediate wrath. But it was a Friday afternoon, and I lived the weekend from hell, in terror of what Monday morning would bring. I could not speak to my parents about it, since they also expected me to know the same damn prayers. There was no escape – or so I thought. Lady Luck had another surprise for me though. I had not taken into consideration the teacher's extreme dislike of Father Carmody. Her simple thinking process yielded a lucky outcome for me. Based on the old maxim that "my enemy's enemy is my friend", she had convinced herself that the priest was the one at fault for the entire debacle. "Father Carmody confused you on Friday evening", she said to me on Monday morning, one of the few times I can remember her actually being merciful to any of us. I was like Superman – once again, with one bound, I was free!

A young lad whom I shall call Simon Kennedy (not his real name) ran into difficulties similar to mine one day when the teacher tasked him with reciting some prayer that he was supposed to have learned off by heart. Clearly he had not done his homework, failing badly to recite the prayer in question. When she asked him why he had not learned it, he replied with one of the oldest but least believable excuses of all, namely, "The page is missing out of my prayer-book". She called his bluff, demanding that he produce the faulty document. He went back down to his front-row desk to retrieve it, and from behind him, many of us could clearly observe Simon's frantic efforts to quickly find the right book, locate the relevant page in the book, and then quickly rip it out, all without being noticed by the teacher. He was asking too much of himself. She was wise to his game, and caught him red-handed. Being unable to recite a prayer was bad enough for a start. Destroying a schoolbook was regarded as a serious matter. But to inflict such damage on a holy book, now that was a crime amongst crimes, residing at the highest level of malpractice. Even worse still, he had lied about it. Her anger was so fierce, we feared she might actually kill him. Simon Kennedy was small, but he was made of tough stuff and somehow he survived the day.

As you may gather, we all lived in fear of the teacher. All except one, that is. My older sister, Anne, a spirited individual, held no such fear. No matter how much the teacher punished her, she adamantly refused to cry, infuriating Mrs. Callinan, and driving her to greater and yet greater lengths of intimidation, attempting to break down Anne's resistance. There was no breaking her, though, and eventually, after some years, Mrs. Callinan gave up, unequal to the struggle. After that, Anne could do more or less what she wished – and she did. She rarely arrived into school earlier than 11AM. Sometimes, if she felt she was likely to be really late, even by her own relaxed standards, she would take my mother's bicycle and cycle to the school. To my knowledge, nobody else ever brought a bike to Moyrhee school. If anyone else was late, they would have to account for themselves, but not Anne. She simply strolled in at her leisure and took her usual place, paying little attention to the rules the rest of us were expected to abide by. This was brought home to me very clearly one particular morning when, as the rest of us were getting ready to head off to school, I realised I did not feel very well, and so, I said the magic words to my mother:

“I have a pain in my stomach”. This could mean anything, a broken leg, diarrhoea, or just a head cold.

My mother replied with her magic words: “Oh, well, you can stay at home so”.

The others left for school.

Later on, a terrible thing happened – I began to feel better. We were reared to be honest and always tell the truth, and like a fool, I did so.

“I’m alright now”, I said.

To which my mother replied:

“Oh, you can go to school so”.

I was horror-struck. What was she thinking? How could I face into school late – and alone? I said nothing, but she must have seen something in my face, because then she came up with a brilliant brainwave:

“Sure, you can go school with Anne”.

Anne! I’d forgotten she even existed!

She was still in bed, of course, but eventually, she sauntered downstairs, and had a wash and a leisurely breakfast. Then we went to school together. I was still a little anxious that we would be segregated on arrival and that the teacher’s wrath would be visited on my head. However, I need not have had any such fear, as I was under protection. Anne saw me right to my desk and then proceeded to hers. There was not a word from the teacher. Now that’s what I call having a big sister.

At school, a great deal of time and effort was put into preparing us for various church events, such as First Communion and Confirmation. A pupil we shall call Peter (that was not his real name) was being questioned by Mrs. Callinan, testing his knowledge of the fundamentals of Catholic teaching. Peter was by no means a star student, so she kept the questions at a very basic level; "Now, Peter, what kind of people go to heaven?" This was far too difficult for Peter, so she began to prompt him. "It's the goo.., the goo.." But it was no use; she had to finish it for him, informing him that the answer she sought was "the good people". So, she tried another question, one that she hoped even someone with Peter's limited knowledge of theological matters could cope with. "So, Peter, what kind of people go to hell?" Once again, Peter was nonplussed. And once again, she prompted him. "Well, Peter, isn't it the ba.., the ba..?" With a joyous burst, Peter realised he had the answer; "The bastards!"

The whole First Communion thing was apparently meant to be a day of celebration. For me, anyway, it was a day from hell. As usual, there was lots of prayer involved and as you may have gathered by now, this was not one of my strengths. There was a prayer to be said before Communion, and another to be said after it. There had also been prayers before and after First Confession. I confused them all. Unlike Frank O'Connor, I have no recollection at all of First Confession. I can only assume that the experience was so terrifying, I must have mentally blanked it out. It's better that way. Our home was in the parish of Tubber, but Moyrhee School was located within the neighbouring parish, Ruan. So, on the actual day of First Communion, the entire event occurred, not in our own familiar local chapel in Tubber, but in a church building that I had never before attended, in Ruan. Twenty-odd years later, Connie and I were married in the same place, and I was shocked at how it appeared to have greatly shrunk in size. But, on First Communion day, because it was not our usual church, and especially because it was a good deal larger by comparison, I may as well have been dropped into St. Peter's Basilica. I was completely overwhelmed by everything. Adults are frequently not aware of how the world that they are so accustomed to is not geared towards little people, who can become utterly intimidated in such circumstances. I certainly was. I did not even know which way I was supposed to face. In today's world, parents are always right there with their children whilst ceremonies of this nature are taking place. But as soon as we got inside the church building, those of us who had been selected for execution, sorry, excuse the slip of the tongue there, of course I meant selected for First Communion, were separated from our families, and corralled into a specific seating area. To further exacerbate matters, our teacher was in the row of seats directly behind us, ready to deliver a sharp dig in the back any time your behaviour failed to match up to her expectations. She would hiss commands in the manner of a viper, spitting venom. Turning your head to look around and try to get your bearings, for example, would be a real provocation to her. I have very little memory of the actual ceremony itself. I do recall that we were required to hold in our hands, a prayer-book of some kind, some flowers, I think, and possibly something else as well, maybe a candle or a rosary beads, or other religious type of object. I was in abject terror of dropping these items, visualising them rolling away from me and disappearing for ever under the surrounding pews. It was indeed a day of terror. Afterwards, people would greet you, congratulate you, perhaps even give you money. They meant well, apparently assuming that one was enjoying the time of one's life.

I remember almost as little from my Confirmation Day, which came a few years later. Being that little bit older by then, I believe I was not terrified to quite the same degree. Prior to the actual day, we were subjected to a form of religious examination, when the bishop and his retinue called to the school. The most unforgettable aspect of this was the whole ring-kissing fiasco. Yes, this was a real thing. The bishop wore a large ring – on one of his fingers, let me hasten to add. As he entered the school gate, we were lined up on each side like some kind of guard of honour. He held out his hand and each of us in turn was obliged to kneel, yes, kneel, and kiss the ring. There is something seriously loathsome about the entire concept of a child having to kneel and kiss the outstretched ring-bearing hand of a much older individual. This was immediately followed by the question and answer session. In the preceding months we had been coached by the teacher for hours, day in and day out, in preparation for just this event. No stone was left unturned in making certain that whatever obscure question of Catholic beliefs was thrown at us by the bishop on the day, we could respond with the correct reply. We were always led to believe that if our responses to this cross-examination did not match up to expectations, then terrible consequences would inevitably follow; namely, anyone who failed the test would not be permitted to proceed with their Confirmation. What difference to one's subsequent life this would make was never adequately outlined. Life without Confirmation; the concept was held to be so awful that I suppose it simply defied description. There was an aspect to the entire examination procedure that puzzled me. The teacher had long since divided the group for Confirmation into two separate cohorts. Cohort A, as we shall call it, since we did not have titles as such, consisted of those of us whom she regarded as capable of handling the pressure of questioning under the gaze of no less a personage than the bishop himself. Then there was Cohort B; these were fellow-pupils who were also the appropriate age for Confirmation, but who, in the teacher's opinion, were unlikely to perform at a high level under questioning. To put it simply, they were likely to fail. During the months of preparation, some pupils who were 'on the edge' as it were, in terms of their knowledge of religious matters, would occasionally find themselves promoted to or demoted from the A and B groups. It was quite similar to promotion and relegation in a sporting league, I suppose. While those of us in the A group were being grilled by the bishop and his sidekicks, the B group were taken into the teacher's private room where they were questioned by a member of his touring group; a priest, I believe. The questions that were put to them were a lot easier than what we were asked, apparently. So, for example, they might get an easy one such as 'Who made the world?' – basic stuff for any Catholic child of the time. At the same time, we were expected to rattle off the likes of 'The Eight Beatitudes'. Fair enough - up to a point anyway. Everyone was put in a situation where they could perform at a level that was perceived to be comfortable for them. Yet it just seemed peculiar to me that if one was expected to perform at a specific level in order to proceed with Confirmation – whatever that really meant – how could it be that two different levels were permitted? Could I not elect to join the 'easy' group? I did not begrudge Cohort B their easy ride; I just wondered why we had to handle the pressure of memorising all the advanced stuff, yet the members of the other group would be allowed to proceed anyway, without achieving the same degree of proficiency. I did not really understand what I was feeling at the time, and I certainly could not express it, but it's clear now that I was feebly beginning to see through the completely false nature of the entire procedure. Or was it the case that my suspicions were unfounded, and the real answer was that the members of my group got a 'Class A' Confirmation, whilst the others have heroically managed to struggle through life with just the 'Class B' version?

The one and only feature of Confirmation that we totally understood was 'The Pledge'. Part of the ceremony involved each of us undertaking a solemn oath stating that, from that day onward, we would never let as much as a single drop of alcohol ever pass our lips – this was known as 'the pledge'. Francis had already prepared me well for how this matter was to be handled. He had long before informed me that the very first thing he did on returning home after his Confirmation ceremony was to sneak into the parlour, and take a good long draught from the bottle of sherry that my mother kept in a cupboard, put aside especially for the very rare visitor who might request such a thing. I do not recall any caller ever asking for or being offered sherry; consequently, the bottle lasted for quite a long time. There's a good chance that it was the very same bottle that I, in turn, slaked my Confirmation thirst with, no more than an hour or so after making 'the pledge'. This oath-breaking activity was concealed from our parents, of course, and for a very practical reason that had little to do with religion. On the rare occasion, such as Christmas, when we were treated to celebratory drinks, the favourite tipple of us children was always lemonade. But pre-Confirmation, it was often the case that you would be strongly encouraged to drink Guinness – or 'porter', as it was known. For some inexplicable reason, adults had been indoctrinated with the belief that porter was a healthy drink for young children. I hated the stuff. I longed for a 'normal' treat such as lemonade, which all the 'post-Confirmationers' enjoyed, while I suffered with my glass of porter. So, from the day I was confirmed I could now enjoy lemonade or orange or whatever non-alcoholic beverage was on offer – as long as my parents were unaware that I had already broken the pledge, of course.

As part of our religious education, we were required to be familiar with the contents of the Bible. I found the stories of the Old Testament were quite interesting, to such an extent that at home, when I was desperate for something to read, I would sometimes take down an old Bible and scan through it. I considered the New Testament to be quite dull by comparison. Silliest of all were parables, which made no sense at all. Take, for example, the tale of the Prodigal Son. Because he went off, had a good time, neglected his parents and then returned when it suited him, he was rewarded with the famous 'fatted calf' and so on. By comparison, the poor guy who stuck around and did his duty was treated with scathing contempt. And this was meant to be a lesson to all of us – so much for Christianity. And as for the Lost Sheep; imagine going off to find one missing animal and then returning to find that the remaining ninety-nine have probably been torn apart by wolves in the meantime. Stupidity is not an adequate word for it.

Walking the half mile or so to school each day was a reluctant pilgrimage. As we rounded the last turn by Joe Roughan's house, the yellow gable end of the school building would just come into view. Every day we hoped that there would have been a fierce fire during the night, leaving nothing but collapsed ruins with maybe just some tell-tale thin wisps of smoke still rising to the sky. It never happened, of course, but in a sad irony, many years later, Joe Roughan's own house did go on fire one night, and poor Joe, a quiet gentleman, perished in it. He was dying of cancer anyway, and being overcome by smoke possibly eased his passing from this life. Closer still to the school building, there was an old signpost at the side of the road warning drivers that there was a school nearby – as if everybody did not already know. After all, almost every single driver on our little road would have attended that same school in their own day – they knew where the building was. The school signpost was not the 'modern' one indicating a small girl and boy walking together. It was the much older type, bearing, in a supremely ironic touch, the symbolic indication of learning, a flaming torch. I suppose it was meant to fire the imagination; to me it meant that all hope was now lost. We dreamed that the teacher might meet an untimely end at the hand of some crazed individual, and, quite incredibly, it nearly happened. This amazing story is not made up; the court records exist. Our teacher, Mrs. Callinan, lived in the schoolhouse. She was separated from her husband, who lived just a couple of miles away. To us, he was something of a mysterious, practically invisible individual. In the afternoons he would arrive at the school, and spend some time outside, chopping firewood. This was one of the two sources of heat for the building, the other being turf. I never remember actually seeing the man, but you would know he was there, as you would hear the steady thumping sound outside as he used an axe on the wooden stumps. Every two years or so, the school exterior needed to be painted. I believe the teacher arranged this herself, usually hiring some local man to do the job. One year, when the painting was complete, it appears that she and the painter in question had words; nobody really knows what happened between them. In any case, he returned later that evening, bringing a large knife with him. It would appear that he came with the intention to inflict harm upon her. Fortunately for her, she was out visiting a neighbour when he arrived. Her unfortunate husband, though, was on the spot, chopping firewood as usual. Again, nobody knows for certain how it came about, but the upshot of events was that the teacher's husband was stabbed, and lost a lot of blood. He did survive and lived on for many years, as did the perpetrator, although, in his case, a number of those years were spent behind bars. Naturally, when we heard the news, we simply could not believe the incompetence of the attacker. He had one job to do and he failed to do it. Once again, our dreams had been shattered. It's extraordinary to think that Mrs. Callinan twice escaped death by cutting. One of my fellow pupils and I occasionally discussed what were the likely chances of being able to do her in ourselves – and how to get away with it, of course. He had it on reliable authority that you could easily construct a bomb using a mixture of sugar and petrol; both readily available commodities. We were of the opinion that the best place to put the bomb would be underneath the teacher's chair, since she spent so much time in it. Also, it would be likely to have maximum effect in that location. How to get the bomb in there without her noticing anything strange – now that was the really difficult part. We knew it was idle talk, really. There was little option but to stick things out to the bitter end, and so, in time, the bomb was, well, dropped, as it were. It looked like Mrs. Callinan would outlast us all, and, indeed, she survived until the school was eventually closed for good. She left the locality and we never heard of her again.

Perhaps my account of our time in Moyrhee School thus far has all the marks of a tale of unending misery and gloom. But it was by no means all bad and we learned to make the best of the situation. Our so-called "play-hour" was typically only about twenty-five minutes long, so there was no time to waste. Lunch was wolfed down rapidly and we quickly burst out the door, unless the rain was absolutely relentless. We had full and free access to all the surrounding territory of fields and crags. The moment we departed the immediate environs of the schoolhouse, the teacher absolved herself of all responsibility for our welfare and did not seem to care where we went. It suited us fine like that. I loved the games, most of which were simple but exhilarating. The most basic of these sometimes consisted of activities as primitive as "pulling down" or "pushing down". Two teams simply pulled or pushed each other on the side of a small hill until the opposing side had been entirely vanquished. Playing "cars" was as basic as running up and down, pretending to drive, and being pulled in by a "guard" who might ask for tax and insurance. That got boring rather quickly. Slightly more sophisticated was a version of tug of war where membership of one side or the other was determined by answering the whispered question "Which would you rather, run a mile or eat a barrel of green snots?" The choice seems ridiculously unbalanced now, but at our age, I suppose a mile must have seemed like an enormous distance to run. My favourite game of all, though, was "hares and hounds". The "hares" hid wherever they could; there were endless places to do so. The "hounds" had to firstly locate them and then run after them and actually take hold of them. It didn't matter to me whether I was hound or hare - I excelled at both.

There were other regular means of escape from the drudgery of schoolwork. For instance, the school building had no running water, and so we would be sent to a nearby well with a bucket to fetch water, mainly for the teacher's own private use, since she actually lived in the schoolhouse. This was always a two-person job and we made sure to take our time about it. It has only just now occurred to me that the two who were sent on this particular mission were always two boys. Apparently, girls were regarded as incapable of transporting a bucket of water, even between two. Another temporary escape was to be chosen for the important mission of making up ink for the inkwells. Yes, this was the 1960's but we still dipped our pens in ink to write. Outside the school environment, ball-point pens, or 'biros', were widely used, but, of course, were completely forbidden where they would have been handiest - in school. Ink was created by adding some special blue powder to water from the rainwater-barrel outside in the yard. The relative quantity of water to powder did not appear to greatly matter. We just made it good and blue and nobody ever said "It's too inky", or "It's too watery". Part of the fun was that your hands would be covered in blue ink for the rest of the day. Our pens were really very crude devices, little more advanced than writing with a quill. At the top of the plastic holder or handle, and yes, plastic had arrived in a big way, there was the metal "nib". This was the part that touched the paper and created the letters on the page. It was sort of pointed and had a split in the middle; I still don't know what the purpose of the split was. Nibs regularly broke so you needed to have spares. You dipped the nib in the inkwell, wrote a few words, and then replenished the nib again with more ink. Refilling the inkwells was another task that involved a degree of responsibility. A shaky hand and there would be ink spilt all over the place. Writing in this way often led to messy results, especially if your pen's nib was on the way out. A spill of ink on the page was a "blot", and a blot had to be dealt with by the use of "blotting paper", a special soft paper the sole purpose of which was to soak up unwanted ink spills. Some years ago, in the 1990's, I was addressing a group of people much younger than me, and I happened to recommend the use of blotting paper for some purpose, that I cannot now recall. Not one of them had ever heard of blotting paper. When I replied that it was for soaking up blots, they then asked me "Yes, but what is a blot?" I should have mentioned the expression "blot on the landscape", but it did not occur to me at the time.

Another very occasional escape from school attendance occurred every five years or so with the holding of an election, or a referendum. The school was used as a voting centre, and so we got a day off. I don't know if it was generally the case that venues as small and as isolated as our tiny school were used as voting centres all around the country, but if it was, then there must have been a very large number of such polling locations. The surrounding population was quite small and I imagine that all the votes would very easily have been accommodated in just one ballot box. That really was democracy at work, I suppose. I also remember that in the weeks coming up to election time, aspiring candidates would appear after Sunday morning Mass, appealing for votes. There were no fancy public address systems or anything of that sophisticated nature. The guy - and it was never a woman - would simply hop up on to the wall directly across the road from the church, where the after-Mass congregation were already assembled for the customary Sunday morning gossip session. He would deliver his oration in as loud a voice as possible. Even though I did not understand a single word of what these men had to say for themselves, I have to say that I always found the event fascinating and exciting. At least it was something different. They seemed so much more committed to their cause, whatever it was, than the priest we had just witnessed completely losing his audience inside the church. If only they could have swapped places. I believe it is true to say that in those days, people were generally more tolerant and patient, and so there was very little if anything in the way of heckling, never mind abuse. One would pity the naïve politician that would have the nerve to attempt such a thing in today's world.

The school photograph was another occasion where we got to leave the drudgery of schoolwork behind, even if it was only for a half-hour or so. As far as I can remember, I believe it only took place every second year. The photo was always taken by a professional photographer and consequently the quality of the images is very good. The version that was taken when my Dad was attending the same school one hundred years ago is not quite up to the quality of those from the 1960's, but, even so, it's not bad at all. Looking back at those pictures now, it is interesting to consider how misleading photography can be, and not just in these days of digital manipulation. A close look at any of the photos in question will reveal that almost all the pupils are really well turned out; nice clothes, hair neatly trimmed, shiny shoes and so on. A naïve chronicler of times past might construe that families were not as badly off in decades gone by as they had been led to believe. This would be wrong, and the reason for it is very simple. We all knew in advance exactly what day the photographer was due to attend, and consequently, our parents (well, alright, our mothers) made sure that we were dressed in our 'Sunday best'. These were certainly not the clothes we normally wore to school every day. Also, in fine Summer weather, it was commonplace for many children to not even wear shoes to school. This would never be allowed to happen on the day of the school photo. We were all much more smartly turned out than would normally have been the case, thus giving quite the false impression. Furthermore, for the relatively small number of children who simply did not possess any 'good' clothes as such (and there were such families), they looked as raggedy as always, and thus the contrast between the better–dressed ones and the poorest ones was stretched well beyond the norm.

Another "let-off" for us during the school day often happened later in the afternoon when the teacher, presumably worn out from her efforts, simply gave up trying to teach us anything and took time out to read and write letters. Mostly, then, we did nothing. We sometimes wondered who she wrote to and who was writing to her; we never found out. She would occasionally fall asleep sitting in her chair by the cosy open fire. She was guaranteed to remain like this for at least a half an hour or so. We kept as quiet as we could, hoping that she would not wake until it was time for us to go home. On one unforgettable occasion, a girl in my class called Marie Baker, embarked on what the rest of us feared would be a doomed mission. With astonishing courage, she crept from her desk right up to the little table in front of where Mrs. Callinan sat. Then she got on her knees directly in front of the sleeping teacher. She raised her joined hands as if in prayer, and remained so for several minutes. We held our breaths, awaiting the explosion of violence that was sure to follow. I'm not certain what exactly Marie had in mind, but it resembled nothing more than a pastiche of an apparition in Lourdes, or maybe the Annunciation, or something along such lines. I'm sure you have seen pictorial representations of the type of thing I mean, with a young girl on her knees before a heavenly visitor. Of course, the big difference was that instead of the apparition being a gloriously beautiful woman, it was a scary-looking old lady, with sticky-out hair, and the complexion of a turkey cock. After what seemed an eternity, Marie rose from her knees, crept away, and returned safely to her desk as though nothing had happened. It's still one of the bravest things I have ever witnessed.

Marie was just one member of the large family of Bakers. I'm not sure how many there were altogether, as some older members had attended Moyrhee School before I had, and some more came after me. As a family, they were unique for two reasons; one, their Dad, who worked in England, was thereby absent for a great deal of the time, and two, they travelled to and from school cross-country, even over a river on the way, by courtesy of a 'coisceim' (the Irish term we used for stone steps set into the water, specifically for the purpose of getting from one side to the other). When the river flooded, they were obliged to go round by the road; a much longer journey for them. One of the Baker boys, Eamonn, and I spent many afternoons towards the back of the room happily chatting and joking whilst Mrs. Callinan snoozed the time away.

The scenario described above, whereby the teacher slept through the afternoon, sitting comfortably close to the warm open fire, while the rest of us froze at our desks, was replicated, apparently, in many other schoolhouses throughout the country. Our families were even required to make a payment towards the annual supply of turf that was stacked at the rear of the schoolhouse. During the school day, in winter, we were regularly sent out to the stack in order to fetch more sods of turf to replenish the fire. In essence, we participated in every aspect of the procedure, bar one; that is, actually benefitting from the heat that emanated from the fireplace. Indirectly, though, there was one beneficial side-effect from the wood and turf-burning open fire. In wintertime, instead of being equipped with a bottle of milk to be consumed with our lunch, we were sent to school with a bottle of tea. Yes, as if our mothers didn't already have enough to do in the morning, they also filled tea into bottles for us, including, of course, added milk and a substantial quantity of sugar, as was the norm in those times. These bottles were placed carefully on the 'hob', a flat area each side of the schoolroom fireplace. Depending on the degree to which the fire had been fed with turf, the bottles could be dangerously hot when the time came for lunch. You would have to let it cool down firstly, thus wasting precious 'playtime'. Occasionally, the heat from the fire would prove to be too much, expanding the liquid within the bottle to such a degree that, if room had not been left inside the bottle for expansion, it would suddenly burst, accompanied by a loud explosive sound. This was exciting for us of course, though you hoped it was someone else's bottle, not your own. These occasional explosions seriously annoyed the already rather easily-annoyed teacher, as she was put in danger of being scalded by flying hot tea, not to mention flying shards of hot glass. Of course, we had little sympathy for her; after all, it served her rightly for sitting so close to the fireplace and hogging all the heat to herself.

Yet another task that, as far as I can remember, was reserved for boys only, was being sent out to cut down a stick for the teacher's use. I don't mean a walking-stick or a stick for the fire; I mean a stick that would be used to beat us. The burning sting from a swiftly swung stick as it impacts on the soft skin of a small child's hand is something that may not leave a physical mark for very long; but the deeper marks are there forever. To try and lessen the severity of the impact, pupils had tried every trick in the book innumerable times. For example, you could suddenly drop your hand just as the stick bore down, thus moving with it, and thereby reducing the momentum of the blow. But that sort of thing just made her madder. Then she would hold your hand in place with one of her hands while she smashed down even harder with the stick in her other hand. There was no way out. On a whim, she might just decide to whack you on the side of the head with her open hand. The impact of that could almost stun you. Also, there is something truly offensive about a skin-on-skin attack; there is no doubting that you are being punished in a very personal manner, and so the feelings of shame, helplessness, anger, resentment and humiliation are even greater than usual. Once, as she dealt me such a blow, her ring caught me just above the eye and left a cut on my forehead. I showed off the scar with pride for some days. I almost hoped that I might lose an eye, becoming famous in the process, but, disappointingly, it cleared up rather quickly. The stick sometimes broke, I suppose from excessive use, and so needed occasional renewal. We have all heard stories of harsh regimes where the condemned person is forced to dig their own grave before facing the executioner; in a similar vein, it was sometimes the case that you were sent out to bring back a stick that was then to be used for your own chastisement. The school was located in quite rough countryside, so there was no shortage of material suitable for the purpose. For example, there was a great deal of hazel conveniently growing nearby. A hazel rod was the teacher's weapon of choice, although I believe an ash plant would have sufficed also. When fulfilling a mission of this nature, there was no use in trying to cheat or outwit her in any way. To return with a half-rotten stick, or one that was impractically long or short, would just amplify her wrath beyond the unacceptable level she had already attained. I recall an occasion when she treated every single pupil in the school in turn to a slap of the rod. I can even recall the question we all failed to properly answer. It was, "What is the Irish word for being 'awake'?" I was by then one of the oldest students in the school, and I was the last to be interrogated. As it happened, I was the only one who roughly knew the word, except I had it slightly wrong, perhaps the declension of it or something. In any case I received the same treatment as everyone else. The stick actually broke in two as she whipped it down on my outstretched palm. Later, I picked up one broken half from the floor, put it in my schoolbag and brought it home. Later still, I felt it was a hateful object to have about the place, and so I placed it where it truly belonged – in the fire.

By this time, being, as I said, one of the senior pupils in the school, there were only two members of our family still attending Moyrhee school; just me and my sister Rose, who was a few years younger than me. Mrs. Callinan was not over-burdened with huge intelligence, but she did possess a malevolent type of cunning, and she did not hesitate to deploy this in turning family members against each other. Whenever she felt that I was not doing enough homework – and I always did just the bare minimum – she would turn to Rose and interrogate her to find out how I was spending my evenings. Rose was far too young and naïve to have learned the subtle but vital distinction between "telling the truth" and "*always* telling the *whol*e truth". The more years you had spent in the school environment, the more you learned about not telling the full truth to the teacher all the time, if, indeed, at all. That's education for you. Rose told her the truth, namely that I spent a good deal of my time reading library books. I'm sure that most teachers today would be delighted to know that their pupils were occupied in this manner. But our teacher took it to mean that I was wasting valuable time that would have been more productively spent with schoolbooks rather than with library books. Overall, though, I have to say that the effect was beneficial, as I determined that from that point onwards I would consume even more library books than before.

Once I had learned to read, I soon developed a love of books. Luckily, I lived in a house that had lots of them, and this was augmented, as mentioned above, by a regular supply of library books. A kind of tradition of bringing home two library books each week (two is all you were allowed), had been started years earlier by my oldest brother James when he attended secondary school in the nearby town of Gort. Then Francis took over during his time at school there. Finally, it was my turn and at last I could choose my own books. The library in Gort was then just a room in a regular house on the main street. It was run by the woman of the house, Mrs. Brennan, whose son Brian was a colleague in my class at school. I thought it must be ideal to live in a house with a library included, but Brian had no interest in it. On one occasion, whist visiting the library, I encountered one of my teachers from school there, a priest called Father Walsh. He immediately took the opportunity to introduce me to the works of Nevil Shute, who he regarded as the greatest living writer in the English language. He had a personal arrangement with Mrs. Brennan that ensured the Shute novels were always located in a specific location in the room, at the front and quite low down, where most people would never see them. I certainly never had. I think that setup suited him. I read a few of them just to keep him happy. At least one of them, "On the Beach" was made into a movie. They are largely forgotten now.

I read everything that was available, including much that I did not understand, as some of the books were clearly intended for an older cohort of readers. I loved to read about crime, detectives and court cases, even though terms such as 'the plaintiff' and 'the prosecution' were a mystery to me. I don't know why but it never seems to have occurred to me to simply use a dictionary. I developed the habit of reading everything that had printed text on it, even including the packaging and printing on food products. Right to this day, for example, I still cannot bring myself to taste a glass of wine until I have firstly consulted the label on the bottle and gleaned as much data as I can in relation to the alcohol percentage, the fruit flavours involved, and so on. Much food packaging now yields a treasure trove of data about calorie content, not to mention salt and sugar etc. In some cases they are even colour-coded like traffic lights; green means good to go, but too much red, well that's meant to stop you in your tracks – or else learn to live with the guilt.

The information is really of little use to me as I will invariably have forgotten it all by the time the meal is finished. As a schoolboy, I even liked schoolbooks. One of the more exciting days of the school year was the day that our new books for the coming year arrived. Unable to wait, I would consume the whole lot the very first evening. The only difficulty with that was, of course, that the books soon became extremely boring, so that by the end of the school year, I had learned to hate them. But then, a new lot would arrive.

I sometimes helped out other pupils with their schoolwork; without the teacher knowing anything about it, of course. After school, it was customary to spend a few minutes with a friend of mine just outside the school gate, but protected from the teacher's view by some convenient overhanging roadside bushes. I would quickly complete whatever maths questions (or "sums", as we simply called them) he had been set for the following day. In this way, he would avoid a tongue-lashing from her the following morning. Either she was not smart enough or did not care enough to dig deeper and ask him how exactly he managed to get all his sums right every morning, even though his other work throughout the day generally did not match up to the perfect score I consistently tried to make sure he got. Another pupil would actually pass his maths exercise copybook to me during the school day, shortly before he was due to present the completed effort to the teacher for her perusal. Understanding that she expected only a relatively poor standard of work from him, he would request me to "do five sums and have two wrong". I think he was probably much smarter than all of us, including the teacher.

From the schoolroom, and there was just one such room, you could see very little outside, even though the windows were quite large. It almost seemed as though our desks had been strategically placed by sadists in such a way that any connection to nature, such as a view of trees, clouds or birds was entirely discouraged; Wilde's reference to "that little tent of blue we prisoners called the sky" springs to mind. However, as you walked by the front window, on the way to or from your desk, you were afforded a brief passing glimpse of the front yard. This normally presented no better appearance than that of a typical prison yard. However, in the early summer, a lilac tree which grew in the corner of the yard, burst into flower, and helped to bring a welcome sign of the bounties of nature into an otherwise grim scenario. Looking out at the lilac helped to remind one that there was another world out there, a world where the ability to recite the rivers and mountains of the four provinces, through Irish, did not matter a damn. I still like lilac trees, and there is one in our back garden. Viewing it does not remind me of school; it reminds me of looking forward to freedom and long summer days.

One of the final acts for a pupil in their last year in Primary school was what was known as the 'Primary Cert'. Long since abandoned, this was a Department of Education written examination, intended to establish what one had or had not learned in one's years in the system. I think there were just three of us from Moyrhee school doing the exam that year; Mary Brohan, Marie Baker and me. The actual examination was not held in our own school, as we were combined with the students from Ruan village school, where the exam was conducted. The only thing I can remember about the exam is that it struck me as being rather easy – or at least that's what I thought. Not long after this, my younger sister Rose, the only remaining member of our family attending Moyrhee school, left that school for good and continued her Primary education at the school in Tubber village. Moyrhee school was finally closed down, the teacher retired, and I never received the results of my Primary Cert exam. I wonder how I got on.

Recently, as I passed by a preschool near to where we now live, I observed a group of small kids excitedly jumping up and down and running around, as children do. Then I noticed they were all wearing a miniature version of the type of cap or 'mortarboard' that is more usually associated with third-level students celebrating their graduation. The penny dropped; now, they even have graduation ceremonies for those who complete their time in preschool! My first reaction, I must admit, was a bit grumpy, thinking, "Well, isn't that going a bit too far?" But then I reconsidered and changed my mind. Why not celebrate every step along the way? The thing now is that school can be a positive experience for many. We were just so glad to get finished with primary school. There was no particular celebration to mark the occasion, nor would we have wanted it. There was no such thing for secondary school either. One day we sat the final examination and after that we just didn't go to school any more. The same applied at third level. We all said goodbye to each other, and that was it, although, in fairness to the head of the college I attended, he did take two of us for a pint in the Railway Bar in Limerick.

Thinking of the relatively small number of schoolmates I had in that tiny school in Moyrhee, I am reminded that they are not all with us now. Two contacted polio during the epidemic of that time. They survived but with life-changing damage to their bodies. Both passed away in their sixties. Two more that I know of chose to take their own lives. At least one other became a politician, that career cut short by a spell in prison. Many of them, I never saw again. There is no past-pupils reunion. The school building itself fell into disrepair, now almost swallowed up by trees and bushes, gradually returning the entire site back to nature. Little remains with us now but memories and copies of the school photograph that was always taken close to the corner where the lilac tree grew. I wonder if the lilac is still there.

Entertainment

It seems difficult to believe now, but there was a time when there was such a thing as a travelling cinema. Well, it wasn't really a travelling cinema, as much as a fellow with a portable projector and a selection of movies that he would put on in a local venue such as the school or the parish hall. There were cinemas in the towns, of course, and had been for decades, but the so-called 'travelling' cinema saved people the bother of having to travel very far. I remember my parents telling me that years before that again, the travelling cinema actually went around with a large tent, a bit like a circus tent, I guess, that could be pitched in a field pretty much anywhere. Apart from boring documentaries about the Catholic missions in Africa, the first real movie I recall seeing was "A Night to Remember", the 1950's film of the doomed maiden voyage of the Titanic. I even remember, before the movie began, the projectionist giving us a short talk about the Titanic and its fate, assuming, I suppose, that the simple yokels in a remote part of County Clare may not yet have heard of the famous vessel and its tragic end.

The circus came around every year. It was always either Duffy's circus or Fossett's circus. While almost all of the acts were fascinating in their own way, the one that really caught my attention the most was always the trapeze act. Flying high above us, barely grabbing each other by the wrists in mid-air, and walking the tightrope; there was no way of pulling the wool over our eyes. It just had to be done right. In particular, the scantily-clad nature of the female performers added an alluring aspect to the entire ritual. For a small boy growing up in a rural location in Catholic West of Ireland, there was something that appeared slightly 'bad' about them, but at the same time, I knew this was entertainment. And it was 'good' entertainment. With the arrival of television, multi-screen cinemas and, eventually, video player/recorders, the rather old-fashioned circus fell on hard times, and was no longer guaranteed the full attendances that used to be the norm. By the 1970's, the alteration that struck me most was the phasing out of the live band that used to accompany all the various acts, replaced by a simple but highly unimpressive tape-recording. In fairness, I never heard even one other person comment on this particular development, but, for me, anyway, the circus would never be quite the same again.

Television arrived in the early sixties, when I was less than ten years old. From outside our back door you could view, in the distance, the construction of the transmitter mast on the mountain-top at Maghera. Over a period of time we saw it gradually grow higher and higher. In much later years, I would visit the site on many occasions to work on various TV and radio transmission projects. Prior to Maghera's completion you could see TV sets for sale in shop windows in Ennis, with little to view on the screen other than what looked like falling snow. Even when Maghera transmitter became available, for the first few years, there were very few actual TV sets in the locality. On our road there was just a single house that had one and so it became a favourite venue for certain occasions, particularly the annual GAA All-Ireland finals. The house in question would be packed solid for the afternoon. We always went along too, not that I had much interest in the actual proceedings, but it was kind of exciting just to see so many people squeezed into one room. Luckily it was a fairly large room. That's also where we went to see the famous World Boxing Championship fights of that era, featuring legendary names like Sonny Liston, Floyd Patterson and, of course, the most exotic of them all, Cassius Clay. A few years later, our nearest neighbour, Paddy Burnell, got a TV set. By then, there were more of them in the locality, and so the days of huge crowds cramming into a house to view football finals in a kind of community atmosphere no longer happened. Before too long, almost every household had a TV and it seemed like the glory days of television were already over by the mid-sixties.

Dad

I have already mentioned how distinctly different from each other my parents were in various ways. This sometimes manifested itself in their attitudes to how the farm was run. Dad worked hard, but he also liked to occasionally take time out – much to Mam's frustration. Working in the meadow, 'saving hay', was an exercise that seemed to go on all summer long, or at least while the weather was fine. It was hot, sweaty, tiring work, and when the weather was favourable, we would work until about nine o'clock in the evening. Even the customary strong Catholic ban on Sunday work could be disregarded when there was serious work to be done, and in those circumstances, we did not even get a day off. Hayseed went everywhere – in your eyes, up your nose, in your hair, down the back of your neck. I didn't care for it. In the heat of the day, I would dream of going for a dip in the cool water of the nearby river and washing all that hayseed away. And sometimes, at the end of the day, I did just that. The trouble was, by then everything had cooled down and so the effect was not as dramatic as anticipated. You could not win. We never had 'togs', or 'bathing costumes' to be posh about it, always going in the river totally naked. It was not like anyone was going to see us; it was, and still is, a very remote place. One such evening, while bathing in the river, I happened to glance down into the water and, practically at my feet, I observed a large writhing black shiny ball of small eels. I got out of there faster than lightning, and never frequented that part of the river again. Saving hay was relentless as you literally did have to 'make hay while the sun shone'. Occasionally, when the weather broke and rain came, my parents would curse their bad luck, particularly if there was still a good deal of hay that remained to be saved. Little did they know I was secretly hoping for the same rain (not praying, mind you), just to give us a break from the endless drudgery. When the rain came, as inevitably it always would, I rejoiced inwardly, but, of course, maintained an outward composure of dejection, as was expected. Lying and hypocrisy are things that can be learned easily enough, even at a young age.

My brother James told me about one fine day (as they say) that Dad did something extraordinary. It must have been a little before my time, as I do not remember it. It was a typical long hot summer's day and, as usual, they were in the midst of the hay-saving season. There was no reason to think that they would be engaged in any other activity for some time to come. But suddenly, with no warning whatsoever, Dad stopped working. He stuck his hayfork in the ground and declared; "We're going to Lahinch!" If he had said he was going to Pluto, it would not have created any greater surprise. Lahinch meant the seaside, miles away, and an outing normally reserved for Sundays that were not fine enough for anything else. But this was not Sunday. There was lots of work still to be done, and the weather was good. Still, it was not as if anyone in the meadow was going to argue with him. Everyone arrived back to the house, to my mother's utter shock and consternation. When she was informed that a mission to Lahinch was about to launch, she almost passed out. Her biggest issue was all about perception. "But what will the neighbours think if they see us going off to the seaside in the middle of the week, and the hay still on the ground?" she asked. Dad was not taking no for an answer this time. "You can come with us, or stay here on your own" she was told. She went with them.

James told me it was one of the best days he ever had at the seaside in his entire life – a day never to be forgotten.

There were some other positive aspects to working in the meadow. To save precious time, we would not go back to the house for every meal. Mam would bring the food to us. Anyone who has ever eaten like this will know that no banquet table can match the experience of sitting on the ground on a fine day, following hours of manual work, enjoying a well-earned repast. It didn't matter that it was usually just sandwiches and tea. We would have eaten anything, and been glad of it. Sometimes, I would be sent to a nearby well to fetch a can of spring water. This had the double benefit of providing an opportunity to drink as much cool water as you liked, whilst also gaining time away from the work environment - at least for fifteen minutes or so. Finally, arriving back to the house after nine in the evening, there would be another meal on the table, typically a salad. This was an extra bonus meal really, to finish up the day.

There were other distractions in the meadow too. Frogs, for example, hid out under the still damp hay on the ground, and when you disturbed them, they hopped away. I don't like to say that frogs are ugly, but there is no doubt that they are truly weird-looking. Also, the speed at which they are able to move from one spot to another in a flash, well, that's kind of unsettling to observe. It's just as well they are not the size of a dog – or a horse.

On a hot day in a meadow, you could occasionally witness a small whirlwind. A perfectly natural occurrence, this would actually lift up some dried hay and carry it for a distance before depositing it again, perhaps some fields away. As was to be expected, some older people called them 'fairy' winds. Indeed, considering that practically the entire population of the country were supposed to be 'devout' Christians, it was amazing how much credence some people gave to the power of the so-called 'fairy' world. Even though it seriously impeded agricultural activities, a lone bush in the middle of a field would be left untouched for generations, in the belief that to cut it down would bring the wrath of the 'fairies' on your head. Wandering into a large wooded area after dark was considered folly by some, not just because you could become lost, which you certainly could, but because the 'fairies' would make damn certain that you became completely lost and you could be left walking around in circles all night long just for their amusement.

Summer days were not all about saving hay, as there were many other crops to be attended to, such as cereal crops like wheat, oats and barley. I particularly recall one occasion when we were taking a break, resting on the headland in one of these fields. Dad took a solid piece of straw about a foot in length. It was hollow on the inside apart from being partially blocked at one end. With a pocket-knife he cut six evenly-spaced holes part-way into the straw, along its length. Then he put the end to his mouth and played a tune on it for us. He had made a tin whistle. Well, a straw whistle. He was no great musician, and, of course, the instrument was completely out of tune. Nevertheless, I was amazed. I had never heard of such a thing being done before, nor indeed, have I ever since. Then he just went back to work.

Some of the most laborious farm work involved working on tillage crops such as carrots, parsnips, mangolds, sugarbeet and so on. All these had to be thinned and weeded, and this meant long days on your hands and knees, working your way up and down what looked like the longest drills in the world. Particularly, in hot and dry conditions, the earth seemed to be as hard as concrete. In later times, precision seeding machines dispensed with all that manual labour. No matter how hard I worked, I could never keep up to my brother Francis. By the time I had completed five or six drills, he would probably have done about ten. For years I used to put it down to him being older than me and therefore more experienced. The truth I did not care to accept was that he was simply a better worker than me. I intensely disliked not just the discomfort of the entire business, but also the way the garden soil worked its way under ones fingernails and into every tiny crevice on the palms of the hands. Only recently in life have I accepted something that was so secret to me, I even kept it from myself – namely that I don't like getting my hands dirty. Perhaps people who know me might say, 'Ah now John, sure we always knew that!' The Covid-19 pandemic was almost a positive thing for me, what with all of that extra hand-washing.

Spraying of crops, especially potatoes of which we always had lots, was an essential activity, necessary to minimise the likelihood of crops being attacked by blight. Again, in later years, this was accomplished from tractor-drawn spraying machines. But, just as in most other small farms, we were still doing it the old-fashioned way. Dad walked up and down the fields for days carrying a heavy spraying can on his back, spraying all around him. At the same time, he worked the handle on the side of the copper can, up and down, keeping up the air pressure that drove out the liquid mixture. I guess it was a little bit like playing the uilllean pipes - just without the music, other than the hissing sound of the spray. My job was to fetch buckets of water across the fields from the nearest well, stream or lake. Carrying two full buckets of water any distance is not the easiest work. Then, standing on the headland, waiting for Dad to arrive back for his regular top-up of the spraying can, was quite boring. There are worse ways to spend a day though, it has to be said. The stuff that was mixed through the water was called Dithane 945. I assumed it was long since consigned to the past, but, to my surprise, when I Googled it recently, I found that it is still in use. It is accompanied by all kinds of dire warnings about the danger of prolonged exposure to the spray generated from this stuff. Dad must have inhaled a million gallons of it, with no apparent side-effects.

Dad always wanted to have a telephone in the house. It was more than just wanting a phone, he needed one. In the late fifties, he had taken up a part-time position as an agent for a supplier of agricultural seeds, a job he did for many, many years. He travelled the North Clare and South Galway area widely taking orders for seeds. A phone in the house would have been hugely beneficial, and so he set about getting it. Very few houses in the general area had phones then, and bringing a telephone connection to a remote rural house meant running many more poles and cable. Every year Dad wrote to the Limerick Department of Posts and Telegraphs Inspector who was responsible for the area. And every year the same reply came back, always starting out with the same litany, "A Chara, I regret to inform you..." etc, etc. Finally, in the eighties, things eventually moved on. The annual reply came from Limerick only this time it began, "A Chara, I am happy to inform you..." etc, etc. The letter-writer added that he commended Dad for his stubborn persistence in this matter. The poles were put up, the cable was run and the long-awaited telephone eventually arrived. Unfortunately, by then Dad was almost ready to retire and so did not benefit from it as much as he would have liked to.

None of us ever had a watch, but Dad always seemed to know roughly what time it was. I assumed he worked this out from the position of the sun in the sky, and I suppose that he did, to some extent anyway. But I eventually discovered his real source of accurate time. From the fields you could hear the occasional sound of a train passing by on the Galway-Limerick line, just a couple of miles away. And from the higher ground you could actually see the train. He knew the train time-table, that was all.

Talking of timekeeping, Dad was handy with clocks too, as he was with many things. Sometimes neighbours would bring faulty clocks to him for repair, which he could usually fix. The ironic thing about it was that our own clock always seemed to be either fast or slow - or stopped. This was where radio with its regular time-checks was important. But if, as was sometimes the case, the radio was also out of order, well then special measures were called for. To be on time for weekly Mass was, of course, regarded as sacrosanct. Accurate time simply had to be established, and I guess there was no train to see or hear in the distance on a Sunday morning. In such a situation, somebody was delegated to call over to the nearest neighbours about a quarter of a mile away just to find out the correct time of day. Sometimes that somebody was me. I would do my best to memorise the time the neighbours told me, but then, on the way home, I would begin to get confused; "Did they say twenty *past* eight, or maybe it was twenty *to* eight? Or twenty to *nine*?" And how much time was elapsing while I made the trip from the neighbour's house back to our place? I would arrive home in a lather of sweat, worrying that I might just be making everything worse. But, somehow, it always seemed to work out alright in the end.

Another thing that neighbours would occasionally call Dad for was to deal with a swarm of bees that may have suddenly arrived on their property – usually hanging from a nearby tree. It always amazes me to witness how fearful many people are of honeybees. Yes, they can sting, but not unless you interfere with their business. Leave them alone and they will leave you alone. Dad would simply shake them into a bag and take them home to put in one of his own beehives. Occasionally, his own bees might suddenly decide to leave the hive and would just take off. There was nothing you could do about it, apparently, so a new swarm that was a nuisance for a neighbour was always a gift for Dad.

There was even a neighbour who relied on Dad to cut his hair. The man in question was a notorious miser, and would never dream of visiting a barber. Instead he came to Dad when the growth was out of control. This gentleman would not have been noted for a very high degree of personal hygiene, to say the least of it, and so my mother insisted that the ceremony be conducted outdoors. Dad also cut our hair when we were children, or certainly that of the boys in the family. I cannot say with any certainty how the length of my sisters' hair was taken care of. For this task, Dad deployed manually-controlled hair-clippers. To cut hair cleanly and neatly, this device relied on fast operation in the hands of the user. Dad was skilled at lots of things, but I have to be honest and say that I really hated having my hair cut, as I could feel every follicle almost being pulled out by the roots. Eventually, the time came when I was old enough to be taken to the barbers in town for a proper haircut; a big step toward growing up.

In June 1963, the US President, John F Kennedy visited Ireland. We reckoned there was no way that we were going to get anywhere near this superstar of the times. But Dad worked something out. From reading the reports in the papers, he observed that on the final day of Kennedy's visit, the planned itinerary incorporated a helicopter trip from Galway to Limerick, before embarking on the final leg to his point of departure for the US, Shannon airport. Dad consulted a map and concluded that, on the Galway/Limerick journey, the helicopters would pass almost directly above our home place. He was right. He recommended that we climb to the top of the nearby old Moyrhee tower, or 'castle', as we called it. We had fashioned a large Irish flag - an American flag would have been too much to expect, what with all those stars and stripes. And we waited. Luckily, it was a fine day. Finally, the helicopters arrived; all three of them, flying right overhead us. We waved like mad, assuming that Kennedy waved back, and who knows, maybe he did. In any case, Dad's calculations were spot-on, as usual.

Our encounter with the American president may have been somewhat indirect in nature, but, in 1966, I did get to shake hands with Ireland's own President, Eamonn de Valera. In that year he embarked on a farewell tour of County Clare, the county that had been the constituency he represented in his time as a politician. His motorcade stopped in every town and village. My mother was a long-time de Valera admirer, and she dragged me along to the crossroads at Tubber village to be present with her at the occasion. In the event, it was all very low key. Considering he was someone who had been amongst the founders of the state and at the very top of Irish political life for half a century, the turnout was pitifully small – about half a dozen of us, outnumbered by Dev's own retinue.

The medieval tower or castle mentioned above was located just a couple of hundred meters from our house. It was one of our favourite places to play when growing up. Not after dark, though, when it was seriously creepy, for me anyway. A large section of the winding stone staircase was missing, apparently due to a lightning strike. Many years later, in his retirement, Dad replaced the missing steps by crafting replacements made from concrete. But, when we were youngsters, we got around the missing section by literally climbing up the wall in one of the rooms. It was a somewhat risky exercise, and if any of us had ever fallen while doing so, the outcome might have been tragic. We were lucky - it never happened.

Just thinking about the castle reminded me about the dog licence. Yes, I know it does not appear that they could be related, but bear with me. I assumed that the requirement to licence your dog was something that had long been abandoned, but a quick search online revealed the astonishing truth that, yes, if you have a dog, you are still supposed to have a dog licence. What exactly the real purpose of such a document might be escapes me, I have to say. Needless to say, even though every farmer had a dog, and often more than one, practically no self-respecting citizen had a dog licence in the fifties and sixties. It was a sort of matter of pride and I suppose also a type of 'fuck off' to the system not to have your dog licensed. Also, it would have been seen as a complete waste of money, which it clearly is. If a Guard was seen approaching the house, an operation would be quickly organised to conceal all dogs, and try to prevent them from barking. Of course, the Guards knew that everyone had a dog but they mostly went along with the charade. Most likely, they harboured unlicensed dogs themselves. I distinctly remember one Sunday afternoon we kids were told that a Guard was very likely to call to the house that very day, checking for dog licenses. I know now that this was nonsense as Guards in a remote country location were very unlikely to be active on a Sunday, and certainly not for such a mundane purpose. Our parents advised us that the safest thing to do was bring Lassie to the castle, which was a little more distant from the road, and keep her under our control there all afternoon, until the danger had passed. And, naively, we did just that. It was only recently that the penny dropped for me. It had to have been our parents organising what in other societies would be known as sending the kids to the cinema so that the parents can safely amuse themselves for the afternoon.

Old buildings like Moyrhee Castle, or preferably ones that were much older, were a real fascination of Dad's. On a Sunday afternoon in summertime, when we really wanted to go to the seaside, he would instead take us on a tour of places such as ruined abbeys, old cemeteries and the like. Kilmacduagh, with its Pisa-like leaning round tower was one of his personal favourites. My mother resolutely refused to join such outings, preferring to stay at home rather than spend the afternoon climbing over walls to get to places where no-one had lived for a thousand years. In fairness, Dad had a good knowledge of the history of these places and I suppose we could have learned a lot from him, had we been interested enough to do so. Sometimes, if Mam complained about not getting to more exciting places, he would infuriate her by asking; "Why would you want to go to places like that when you are already living in one of the most beautiful places in the world?" In his later years he edited and contributed to a local history of the area; 'The Parish of Kilkeedy'. He was 86 years old when that book was published. Some of the book's content has now been used in the construction of a website celebrating the heritage of the parish of Kilkeedy. It may be seen at https://kilkeedy.clareheritage.org/

Not too far away from the town of Gort and very close to where my mother had grown up there was another old tower or 'castle' known as Thoor Ballylee. It achieved fame for being the home of W. B. Yeats for a number of years, back in the 1920's. It subsequently fell into disrepair but was restored in the 1960's. There was a big 'opening day' in 1965, I think, which we attended, along with many others. I recall most of us being out on the road beside which the tower is located, but getting nowhere near the actual building itself. My most abiding memory of the day, however, is observing waiters regularly flash by, whisking trays of what looked like flutes of champagne. I had only ever seen this type of thing in the movies. Who was the champagne for? Why could we not have some? In fairness, I was only twelve years old, so it was unlikely that I was going to be offered alcohol. But neither were any of the adults around me. I suppose there must have been an area reserved for so-called 'VIP's', the kind of people who are fawned upon at an event of that nature. It seemed that little had changed despite the passage of time. The class of people who considered themselves to be true aficionados of poetry, architecture and champagne were looked after, whilst the ordinary peasant class, such as ourselves, were left to aimlessly mill around outside, wondering what it was all about, just as they might have done in the 1920's, and before.

Cars were the bane of Dad's life, mainly because he never had a really good one. Even when he was retired and we were in a position to get together and buy him a car, he chose a Mini. It was the last thing I would have recommended, as I'd had one myself, and it gave me a lot of grief. In the sixties he had a series of Ford Anglias, the famous, or infamous, 'notchback' Anglias. Every two or three years or so, when the time came to change the car, he liked to go to Dublin to do so, because, he said, the market of available cars was so much larger there. I suspect he liked to get away to the city for a couple of days really, and who could blame him? The funny thing was, he did not like to drive in such built-up areas, and so he would get the garage people to drive the newly-acquired car out as far as the Naas road for him, ready for the road home. Several of these cars in succession were of exactly the same make, model, and even the same colour, maroon. They were all second-hand and they were all exactly the same, just separated by a few years. Greatly simplifying the paperwork, Dad never actually changed the car at all - officially. He merely put the old number-plates on the newer car. The same tax-book or registration document was used for a decade or so, and the same car was declared for insurance purposes every year. It was all completely illegal, of course, but so what? It was not as if he were ever likely to have an accident. Beginning in 1952 he drove many different cars, all quite slowly it has to be said, for the next forty years or so, and generally without any significant incident. Well, once he told me of an occasion when he was driving along and, to his astonishment, suddenly noticed a car wheel rolling swiftly along the road ahead of him. It took a few moments before he realised that one of the wheels from the car he was driving had come loose and broken away.

One of his favourite things was stuff called Isopon. These days, of course, cars no longer rust, corrode and generally fall to pieces in the way that they did in Dad's time. There were often many holes in the car's bodywork and he filled these with Isopon – to such an extent that we used to joke that eventually a stage would be reached when there was more filler than metal in the car. He became quite expert in every facet of motor maintenance, fixing things that nobody would attempt now. For instance, he never once took the car to a garage to fix a puncture - and punctures were quite a frequent occurrence. He used tyre levers to get the tyre off the rim and to get the inner tube out, to be patched up. Again, we used to joke that there was more patches than original rubber in the tubes. Just once I tried to remove a tyre from a wheel in this way i.e. using tyre levers. I completely failed to accomplish the task, even though I had witnessed Dad doing the same thing hundreds of times. He was both strong and skilled. The quality of the patches and the solution used to attach them was not the greatest though, so that, in very hot weather, the patches could 'lift', thus re-opening old wounds, as it were. For this reason, on very hot days, Dad would move the car to a shady spot under a tree, in an effort to keep the temperatures down. Sometime, when watching Formula I racing, and I see the mechanics preparing the wheels and tyres by wrapping them in electrically-heated covers, I feel like shouting at the screen, "Don't do that! The patches will lift!"

The ironic thing was that, despite his long relationship with cars, he was not really a very good driver. No, he was not reckless, or anything like that, quite the contrary, in fact. Having learned to drive on very ancient machinery from the 1930's, he never moved on to taking advantage of the more developed gearboxes and clutches of the 1960's; certainly crude by today's standards, but silky smooth compared to what he had grown accustomed to. He tended to be a little bit savage with the clutch pedal, and his relationship with the gear lever was more hostile than meaningful. He snatched at the gear-change rather energetically, as though it were likely to run away from his grasp. When we grew old enough to have our own cars, and if Dad's was out of action, he might ask to borrow one of ours. You sighed with relief if it was not your car as you listened to him thrashing the gearbox. In fairness, he had grown up with motorcars that needed to be manually started with the use of a handle stuck into the front of the engine. What young person would believe that today?

He was very patient with us, rarely losing his temper, or even raising his voice. For example, he helped us prepare for exams. One of the few things that would irritate him was if we were making too much noise while the news was on the radio. The radio news irritated me, so we would occasionally come to loggerheads at a time like that. Clearly, he did not hold with any form of corporal punishment, as he never put as much as a finger on any of us. Just once I remember him getting so mad that he ran after me, round and round the table that stood in the middle of the kitchen. I was much lighter on my feet and much faster than him, so it was no contest. Anyway, what would he have done if he had actually caught up to me? Perhaps he had thought this out, and decided to just let me get away with it. He was generally so patient and understanding that you would immediately feel sort of guilty for annoying him even slightly. He always wore a hat outdoors, and as soon as he entered the house, he just randomly flung it down where ever was convenient. Going back out again, he could never find it. "Where's my hat?" he would exclaim. Sometimes Mam would despair and just reply "I suppose it's wherever you left it when you came in". He didn't like that at all and would become even more exasperated. At that stage, rather than exacerbate the situation any further, it was better to organise a hat-hunting party.

Not only was he quite strong and skilled, but he was fit as well, certainly when he was younger. Entering the kitchen on a Sunday morning, as the entire family had just returned from Mass, he would run across the room and with a high kick, just deftly touch the underneath side of the bookshelf above the fireplace with the toe of his shoe. The shelf or mantelpiece in question was almost six feet above floor level. I eventually grew taller than him, but I never managed to accomplish it myself.

All farmers were expected to keep the roadside hedges on their land trimmed right back, and you could be prosecuted for not doing so. I know Dad was fined in court at least once for this so-called 'offence'. The irony is that farmers are now encouraged to let their hedges grow and can actually be prosecuted for excessively cutting them back. So Dad was right all the time. When one-way streets were firstly introduced in the town of Ennis, he was in court again, for driving the wrong way. The judge let him off without a fine, saying "Ah, sure, the system is new, you weren't used to it". However, Dad told us afterwards he had known perfectly well but just took a chance on it and got caught.

He worked outdoors in all kinds of weather, but when it got so bad that even he had to abandon such activities, he found plenty to do indoors. His culinary skills were limited, but if Mam was not around, he would sometimes make toffee. Why would you want a nutritious dinner, when you could have toffee? He also had an interest in photography. On a few occasions he had a go at developing film and producing his own black and white prints. The results were mixed, it has to be said. In a set of photos taken on the day of my First Communion (or maybe it was Confirmation, I'm not sure – the events were pretty much interchangeable, anyway), something went slightly askew during the development process with the result that each print had a double image of me. There was a paperback in the house at the time by Edgar Wallace, once a popular author, now completely forgotten, called 'Double Dan'. Needless to say, I was re-christened 'Double John' for a while, until the novelty wore off.

Mention of First Communion and Confirmation reminds me that it was Dad who took me to the town of Gort to be equipped with a suit of clothes for both of these occasions. Mam always sourced all our other clothes, so exactly why this particular function was fulfilled by Dad, I do not know. Men's clothes shops were known as 'drapers' then; I don't know if the term still even really exists. Another place in the town of Gort that I recall visiting with Dad when I was still quite young was his aunt's house. Gort is really a very small town, and a place that I came to know well in later years, when I attended secondary school there for five years. But when I was little and unused to the urban environment, I may as well have been surrounded by the towering skyscrapers of Manhattan. In the countryside, all houses were either one-storey or two-storey – nobody ever built a house higher than that. But in the town centre, most houses were three storeys high. They were really just standard town houses, but they appeared immense to tiny me. When visiting Dad's aunt's house, she entertained us (meaning tea for Dad and lemonade for me) on the top floor. It almost seemed as if the place was even bigger on the inside than on the outside. At one point she asked me to fetch a letter she had received and that she wanted Dad to inspect. She told me that I would find it on the landing window on one of the lower levels. I located the letter quite quickly, but then was overcome with a sense of sheer dread and panic at the realisation that I would possibly never find my way back to where they were conducting their conversation. It seems ridiculous now, but it did not seem so at the time. Standing in the bowels of what appeared to be a gigantic mansion, I was smart enough to listen out for and to follow the murmur of their distant voices. I got back in no time and they never suspected a thing. This is the first time I've ever disclosed this rather sad confession.

Another hobby that Dad occasionally indulged in was leatherwork. He purchased sheets of leather somewhere – I have no idea where. He would cut this up into sections and typically assemble, for example, a wallet or lady's purse. He used some type of small punch to stamp a pattern all over the article. Unfortunately, to the best of my knowledge none of these examples of his leatherwork have survived. The other thing that he made from leather was a schoolbag that both my older brothers used in turn going to primary school, and which was eventually passed on to me.

He liked to try out growing various different things as well as the usual farm produce. For instance, in the early forties, when tobacco was rationed due to being in very short supply, Dad grew the stuff himself. Of course, our climate is not comparable to that of the American state of Virginia, but necessity can indeed be the mother of invention and some Irish farmers were contracted to grow tobacco plants during that period. I can remember when he grew tomatoes. Producing tomatoes in this climate is not so challenging compared to growing tobacco; I know, having even done so myself. Lacking a glasshouse, or the more modern type of plastic mini greenhouse, Dad fabricated his own version of one. The underlying structure was made from lengths of timber that he cut down himself. On to that he fixed a large number of used plastic fertiliser bags. Admittedly, the entire thing was torn away when the winter storms arrived, but that was after we'd had delicious tomatoes all summer long. It was good of him to go to all that trouble, considering he never ate any tomatoes himself, having a strong aversion to all food that was red. The fruit that he grew and that he took the most pride in were loganberries, which are a cross between raspberries and blackberries. Personally, I found them to be rather bitter.

The concrete floor in the kitchen had begun to crumble away, and so Dad set about laying a new one. Of course, unlike anyone else laying a new floor, he had his own unique approach; he coloured the concrete. He did this by adding some coloured powder to the mix. I have no idea what the stuff was, but I do remember that he used at least three, or perhaps four different colours. As best as I can recall, it was a combination of primary colours, perhaps red, yellow, blue and green. He marked out the floor area, dividing it into concentric squares of different widths. Each successive squared area was made a different colour. The result was magnificent. Sadly, it was not to be one of his more successful projects in the long term. Over a period of time, all the colours faded and everything turned to almost grey again, the once-bright colours ending up close to invisible. Years later, he and I spent a wet day laying floor-covering over the entire area. That was replaced again in more recent times, but I suppose the remains of the coloured concrete are still there underneath it all.

The old range in the kitchen was almost always on the go. We burned mostly timber since there was so much of it about. Sometimes it could prove difficult to get the fire started, and in order to hasten the process, Dad would throw in some paraffin oil. If that did not do the trick, he would use petrol. Please do not try this at home; the effect can be explosive.

Cows had to be milked every single day, morning and evening. It was done by hand before farmers began to install milking machines. Even now, with the most modern milking parlours, it is a seriously demanding treadmill that has to be walked every day by dairy farmers. Luckily for me, I never learned to milk a cow. I'm not sure how I got away with it. Our Dad got up so early every morning for this work that we never even heard him moving around. As we got ready for school, he would come in from his milking labours, having already been working for a couple of hours. He did that practically every day of his life until he retired. The full creamery cans of milk from each farm were collected by a local man and taken to the creamery some miles away. In a sort of barter system that would be unheard of today, each farmer could order butter from North Clare Creameries, and it would be delivered on a regular basis by the chap who returned the empty cans from the creamery. The cost of whatever number of pounds of butter that were ordered was taken from the monthly creamery cheque. It was a really simple but elegant system that worked perfectly. A similar scheme was operated by the Irish Sugar company. Farmers who grew sugar-beet, and we were among them, could order a load of fertilizer from the company, some of which could then be used for the following year's crop. Again, the cost of the fertilizer was taken from the cheque paid to the producer for the sugar-beet. Of course, all four sugar-beet factories were subsequently closed down and now all our sugar products have to be imported. Perhaps there is logic behind that, but if there is, I have never heard it outlined.

Dad worked hard, but he also liked to attempt ingenious labour-saving solutions, some of which I believe were unique to him. If the car simply could not be started, and that was not uncommon, he would try anything to get it going. Apart from getting the entire family to give him a push start, I remember, on really cold days, seeing him extract all four spark plugs from the engine, bring them into the house laid on a shovel which he then heated over the fire in the range. When they were good and hot, he would rush out and quickly re-insert the plugs back in the engine. It didn't always work but it was interesting to watch. For years we had a huge white horse that was very strong and could pull pretty much any weight that was asked of him. Dad would connect the horse to the front of the car, sit in, and with the reins out the window, control the animal until the car started. The horse was so accustomed to this activity he knew to stop pulling when the engine came to life. If only we'd had video cameras then.

I was not aware that our big white horse had a name, though both Gerita and Rose have assured me that his name was Bob. How come I never knew that? Anyway, he was a gentle, docile creature. When he lay resting on the ground, we could approach him and rub his head, just as one would with a dog. As a small child I was always amazed at the sheer size of his enormous head when you were that close to him. He was present for practically all our young lives. He was quite smart too. In the evenings, if he grew tired of the field he had been left in, he would rattle the latch on the gate with his mouth until it opened and he could then take himself to an alternative grazing ground. Sometimes at night, from inside the house you would hear the slow resounding sound of his hoofs as he walked over the stone surface at the rear of the house, moving from field to field, and this time opening two gates. Occasionally, he would wander off the roads to graze the so-called 'long acre' just for a change. There was never any need to go and fetch him. He would always come back in his own good time. I witnessed Dad ploughing with that horse, as well as conducting many other similar jobs. Then when the horse got really old and was clearly approaching the end, Dad took on the type of task that I knew I could never steel myself to, one of the many reasons I could not be a farmer. He took our faithful white horse to the nearest railway station to be transported to some place where they turned old horses into glue, or something of that nature. So we were told anyway. I remember that James went with him on that final journey. I was glad I was not asked to do it. Even now I still find it emotional to think of the way that noble animal departed from our lives.

"Keep a thing for seven years and you will find a use for it" - that was a favourite expression of Dad's. He threw nothing away and, fully acting on his own advice, I'm pretty sure he had some things around the place for seventy years, never mind just seven. Hardware supplies, for example, required a nine or ten mile trip to town, so it was incumbent on farmers to be able to re-use and re-cycle, long before such advice became politically correct. Many, many times I witnessed him re-straightening bent nails with a hammer. An annual recycling event involved preparing for the storage of grain, ready for the visit of the threshing machine or the combine harvester. Jute bags, in which fertiliser had been delivered earlier in the year, were used for this purpose. But firstly they had to be cleaned – you didn't want fertiliser mixed in with your oats or barley. So, a job we kids were given every year was to take the jute bags to the stream and wash them clean of any trace of fertiliser. We would wade into the stream and swish the bags about until they were clean. It was quite hard work but something I always enjoyed. In later years, the old-fashioned jute bags were no longer used for fertiliser, having been replaced with plastic ones; the familiar plastic bags that became one of the most common and unsightly blots on the agricultural landscape for many years; so much for progress.

Many of the little bits and piece, like nails and screws, for example, that Dad kept around the place, he stored in various tins and large jam jars. He greatly regretted the demise of the "two-pound pot of jam". By comparison, the one-pound jam jars just simply did not measure up when it came to storage space.

Amongst all his many other skills, Dad could handle construction work too. He constructed a new cow-house, practically single-handed. Admittedly, it took him years to finish it, but it still stands there today. Every single bit of concrete was mixed by hand, on the ground. I loved to watch him doing this, as he added water, sand

and cement until the mixture was just right. Nothing was ever measured; everything was estimated by eye and, I suppose, by the heft of the shovel. That structure was barely complete when he set about building a new piggery. This was in the 1960's, but he already knew all about insulation and heat conservation. The theory was, apparently, that pigs thrive better in a warm environment. Who would have thought that such crude animals could tell the difference? Overhead, he filled the roof space, which would normally be left empty in an agricultural building, with large quantities of straw, kept in place with sheets of plastic. We thought he was overdoing things, but I guess he knew what he was doing. The floor was even more interesting. Before putting down the final finish of cement, he covered the entire floor with egg-cartons, thus ensuring that there was an in-built layer of air down there, providing further insulation. We all assumed the egg-cartons would collapse as soon as anybody walked on the floor, but, of course, that never happened.

Soon after a visit to the filling station, Dad found that the car's petrol filler cap was missing – he must have forgotten to put it back on. I don't think it even occurred to him to go and buy a replacement cap. Again re-utilising existing resources, he cut up a 'Batchelors' pea or bean tin, using just the lower inch or so of it, along with the base. You would think it had been made for the job – it fitted perfectly. Perhaps he should have informed the Ford motor company (he had always driven Ford cars) that they didn't need to manufacture petrol filler caps at all, since Batchelors already had a cheaply-made perfect solution on the market.

Not all of Dad's ingenious ideas were as successful. Every year when the harvest was completed, the bags of grain would be stored in what we called 'the barn'. The barn was really just another farmyard shed. Many urbanites are probably familiar with the cliché that states 'you are never more than six feet from a rat'. Apparently it is not actually true, with the average distance to the nearest rat being more like 50 metres. But, in the countryside, if you have quantities of grain stored nearby, then you will certainly live close to rats, and lots of them. Where do they come from and how do they find the grain? I don't know. One year, in what I assume was an effort to out-manoeuvre the rodents, Dad decided to try something different. He stored the bags of grain in the tower or 'castle' referred to earlier, using one of the higher floors within the building. Bags of grain are quite heavy, certainly too heavy to haul up a winding staircase, so he thought out a clever method to get round that. He opened a hole in the floor of the first storey by temporarily removing a large square stone piece. About two metres above this he installed a large wooden beam right across the room. Then by throwing a length of rope over the beam, he and James hauled the bags of grain up through the hole in the floor. I remember watching them, fascinated. So far, all seemed good. But when winter came, quantities of water seeped through the ceiling of the room and dripped incessantly down on to the bags of grain below. A lot of the grain rotted. And what did not rot was consumed by the rats who somehow found their way upstairs to what they must have found to be a delightful and very well stocked dining room, quite undisturbed as a result of being a good distance from the farmyard.

One thing that really stood out about Dad's generation (and Mam's) was their teeth – or, rather, their lack of same. Dental care must have been practically unheard of in their day, as many people in their age group had to resort to wearing dentures relatively early in life. Dad apparently had false teeth from the age of thirteen or so. As I mentioned earlier, our parents passed various good practices on to us, but taking care of your teeth was not one of them. Consequently, I too, lost a number of my own teeth much earlier in life than I should have let happen. I can recall seeing my mother arrive home from the town of Ennis on a wintry day, having cycled the ten miles, following a typical visit to the dentist. She was in agony. This type of thing was not very unusual, but such an event was really put in its place by the activities of my aunt, who apparently cycled a similar distance to Ennis County Hospital to give birth.

Dad could be witty too. When it was reported to him that a neighbouring man who was known for his erratic driving manner and involvement in numerous accidents claimed to have driven a quarter of a million miles without an accident, Dad retorted, "Oh, really? And I suppose he has driven a *half* a million miles *with* accidents!" Once, when we were playing Scrabble, I saw the opportunity to use the word 'sex' (10 points for that). I hesitated because I had never once heard him use the word, and felt he might find it embarrassing. Then I reconsidered, thinking 'well, we are both adults, so what the hell'. I went ahead and put the relevant letters on the board. I need not have worried; without hesitation, he immediately appended the letter 'y' (14 points). I was pleasantly surprised recently to see the same scenario played out on the Disney+ series 'Only Murders in the Building'.

"Go and boil your head" – another of Dad's favourite expressions, especially if you asked him for something that he could not give. There was no malice in it. He would share whatever he had, never coming home to us without a packet of sweets, of which he would have eaten only about half himself. He did have a sweet tooth. He smoked a few cigarettes every day, and when I, as a teenager, began to smoke also, he did not lecture me about it, as one might expect. Instead, he would regularly send me to the shop for 10 Carrolls. From the pack, he would extract three, which he gave to me, retaining the other seven for his own use. This I considered to be an entirely fair arrangement. Ultimately, we both stopped smoking at around the same time; when I was twenty-five and he was sixty-five.

Dad's life was quite tough, but he never seemed to complain about it. There was an occasion, for example, when he was asked to drive to Dublin to transport the ill daughter of relatives to see a specialist in the city. When they arrived in Dublin, it transpired that the family had booked accommodation for themselves, but not for him. He spent the night in the car, before driving them back across the country the next day. He never spoke of it, and it was something I only heard about in recent years, long after he had passed away. In his retirement years, he was able to relax a little, indulging himself more in lifelong passions such as beekeeping. He was stung innumerable times. He wore little in the way of protection from the bees, other than a large piece of muslin over his head and tied around his neck. Bees crawled in underneath it and down his back, stinging as they went. It did not bother him unduly.

During his working years he had rarely ever taken a drink, but in later years he really enjoyed a visit to the pub for a whiskey - or a 'small Power' as he called it.

Once, when Dad was quite advanced in years, I asked him how he was feeling. "Oh, I'm grand", he said. Then, when he'd had a moment to think about it a little more, he added; "Of course, every bone in my body is aching!"

My late sister Anne wrote his obituary, ending with a statement that perfectly summed up the kind of man Dad was: "He was a gentle man and a gentleman."

Mam

Whereas Dad rarely spoke of the past, Mam never seemed to stop talking about it. She often told us about the tough times she and her siblings endured as pupils attending Kiltartan National School, where the teacher was a child-hating sadist. Things got so bad for her brother John that, one day, he took a pen-knife from his pocket, threatened the teacher with it, and then walked out of the schoolhouse, never to return. After that, the teacher gave the remaining members of the family an even harder time of it.

She grew up in an area and at a time when some people believed in the superstitious. She told us stories about people walking home on a dark night and having to stop, because a giant black dog with huge red eyes barred their way, necessitating a diversion to an alternative and much longer road home. And she told us about neighbours who fell out and had a curse put on their farm so that their cows produced no more milk. She further embellished this tale, I think, explaining that a member of the evil family had the ability to turn into a hare and drink the milk directly from the cows of the unfortunate family that was being victimised. Karma was forthcoming though; someone fired a shot at the hare, wounding it seriously. Later on, it was found that a member of the suspect family lay dying from a gunshot wound, complete with a deathbed confession and a desperate last-ditch request for forgiveness. As a young boy, I naturally believed a lot of that stuff and, to be honest, you can never easily forget it.

William Butler Yeats and Lady Gregory frequented the Kiltartan area when my mother was a young girl. She only had good things to say about Lady Gregory who occasionally visited the children in the school and was kind to them. In the case of Yeats, however, they were advised to have nothing to do with him, presumably on the basis that he was known to be (a) not a Catholic, (b) a poet and (c) worst of all, a man who was believed to have had close relations with more than one woman.

When she married Dad and came to live in his house, it was really her first time away from her home for any length of time. Whenever we asked her what it was like in those early days, she explained that all the internal walls in the house were black. I found this quite shocking. Why would anybody deliberately decorate the walls in black? It would be many years later before I discovered that if you ask a child what their first days in school were like they will often give a similar reply i.e. that all the walls were black. It seems to be some type of psychological memory response to the first real separation from home. In any case, she did eventually adapt, and by the time we came along things were not so dark; to my knowledge there is no such thing as black wallpaper.

Amongst my earliest memories of my mother is listening to her sing as she operated the separator. A long-forgotten device now, the separator was used to separate cream from milk. Internally, the device operated at an amazing speed, somewhere in the region of 100 revolutions per second, separating the different liquids through centrifugal action. This was achieved through gearing, the machine being cranked quite slowly by hand. It was quite hard work to get the thing up to speed and to keep it going, but Mam actually seemed to enjoy the experience. The machine itself emitted what you might call a sort of 'singing' sound, I suppose, and she liked it enough to sing along with it. Some of her favourites were songs by Bridie Gallagher, a popular entertainer in the 1950's.

Many farming households also made their own butter, and we sometimes did so too, though the development of the local creamery really hastened the demise of home butter-making. We had a small table-top glass churn for this purpose. Like so many things then, it was manually driven. You wound a handle at the top and the beaters, or whatever they were called, inside turned the contents to butter – but it took what seemed like hours of toil. In reality it was probably no more than twenty minutes or so. Emerging from the churn would be a few pounds of butter, to which my mother added a huge dose of salt. In a lifetime, you will never taste nicer butter than this. But even better was to come. In early summer, when the first potatoes ('early spuds') were dug from the garden and boiled, Mam would mash them, mixing in home-grown spring onions. This was what she called 'pound'. At the table, you would add the home-made butter to taste – meaning almost as much butter as potatoes. Of all the things I ever tasted in my youth, and I even include Christmas cake in this evaluation, there was simply nothing better than 'pound'. If I believed in heaven, I would expect to be served pound there for dinner every day for all eternity. No churning would be required, of course, and there would be zero weight-gain as well.

Mam and Dad did have at least one thing in common; they both had a sweet tooth. However, when it came down to the last few sweets or squares of chocolate, it always kind of surprised me that, despite her fondness for these sugary things, she would inevitably surrender the final ones to us, leaving herself without in doing so. I suppose that is what many mothers do. At the same time, she was hopeless at dividing things up properly. Say, for example, a nice cake had been brought home from town and there were five or six of us waiting expectantly for our share. Had it been Dad slicing the cake, he would logically first count the number of us around the table, and then divide the cake accordingly, in a fair and reasonable manner. Mam dispensed with such troublesome detail; she would simply cut slices at random, all of them different shapes and sizes.

As it became evident that you were going to be one of the last to be served, your heart would sink lower and lower as you observed the remains of the cake quickly diminishing in size. But, then again, you might be lucky and be served first; it was a lottery.

She always believed that she was overweight, though, if she was, it cannot have been by very much, as it did not prevent her from living to the age of 101. Occasionally, she would invest in packs of Ryvita, and go on a so-called 'diet'. Ryvita is a kind of crispy high-fibre low-fat biscuit. I could never understand how eating more stuff could make anyone thinner, and, indeed, it never seemed to make any difference. As soon as the Ryvita ran out, she simply moved on and forgot about the whole thing. There also used to be things called 'diet pills' or weight loss pills and perhaps they are still around. She never took them and actually used to tell a really frightening story about such pills, a story that I think she may have made up. She said that a woman who was taking these pills to lose weight put one in a glass of water at her bedside, intending to take it later on. However, she fell asleep and when she woke up, she observed that the pill was no longer visible in the glass of water, but a little worm could be seen swimming around.

For a fairly heavily built woman, she could move with speed and agility. There was always a four-stone sack of flour in the kitchen, as Mam made bread practically every single day of her adult life. She made the bread in a small round metal basin that she left inverted on top of the sack of flour. Flour inevitably attracts mice, especially in older houses. Sitting by the range in the long evenings, she would occasionally hear the unmistakable scratching sound of a mouse underneath the basin. Armed with the poker from beside the range, Mam would creep silently across the kitchen floor, then quickly whip off the basin, and in a flash she would introduce the unfortunate rodent to the great flour-sack in the sky. Her aim was deadly; I don't think she ever missed.

And another thing Mam would never miss was the Galway Races. It was then a three-day racing festival and she would attend for one day, usually the day of the Galway Plate. She would always take one of us with her. When I was too small to go, I would spend the day watching out for the returnees, knowing they would bring goodies from Galway; rock, for example, and I mean the rock you can eat. Eventually the time came when I was old enough to go too, which I did for a few years. It was a big day out. Early in the day, Dad would drive us to the train station in Gort. Armed with the daily paper, Mam and I would concentrate on the racing section to the exclusion of all else. Anyone would think we knew something about racing. We didn't really, but then neither did about 90% of all the people going to Ballybrit. We would select 'winners', thus saving time for when we would eventually arrive at the actual racecourse. But there was a lot to be done before that. Arriving in Galway, the first destination was always the nearby Woolworths store, straight across from the train station in Eyre Square. Trips to the city were rare, and local towns such as Ennis did not have anything on this scale. The funny thing is I cannot recall ever buying anything there, but I suppose it was the equivalent of somebody from Hicksville travelling to New York and getting to visit Macys or Bloomingdales. On a couple of occasions, well-meaning ladies from the neighbourhood insisted on making the journey to Galway with us, intent on spending the entire day in our company. Mam was not up for this at all. As soon as we all got into Woolworths she would pretend to be exploring one of the shopping aisles, when suddenly she would say to me, "Now, Johnny, come on, we'll give those two the slip". And so we did. That evening, when we met up with them again at the train station for the return journey, she would exclaim, "Oh, God, we lost sight of you. Where did you go at all?" Next we would explore the main shopping street, including the department store that I think was called Glynns. Then it was time for sustenance and there was no better place than Lydons for tea and a monumental plate of delicious cakes. The next item on the agenda was a bus trip to the seafront at Salthill, but not for a dip in the ocean. No, Mam's weakness for gambling machines was given full and free rein in the gaming arcade there. She never won very much, but then she never lost very much either. By this time, afternoon was approaching and the races would soon be starting. Another bus ride was called for, this time to Ballybrit racecourse. The boredom of the long walk from the main road into the racecourse was alleviated by occasional bursts of activity from the 'three-card-trick' merchants. There was always a sucker in the crowd who was prepared to lay down a fiver (a lot of money in the 1960's), confident that he could pick out the right card. Mam warned me never to get involved with these chancers. No warning was necessary really; it was pretty obvious that the punter never won. It was even quite obvious to me that when somebody did occasionally 'win', it was really an accomplice of the villain with the cards. On one occasion, as we entered the race-track general area, Mam spotted a young couple canoodling on the ground nearby. Openly romantic kissing and cuddling of this nature was, for some reason, generally held to be unacceptable to her generation. She made some derisory remark about them, and tried to whisk me quickly by, to ensure, I suppose, that I would not be in some way damaged by the sight of their harmless activity. In any case, it was too late; not only had I seen them, but I also recognised both of them. Finally arriving at the actual racecourse, it was time to place some bets. Mam did not trust any bookie, and so always bet using the Tote only. It did not make much difference; we never won a whole lot anyway. When it was time for the next race to begin, we would make our way right up to the fence, so that the horses passed by within a few feet of us. I was truly staggered the first time I saw, heard – and felt – the powerful sight, and in particular, the sound of a herd of racehorses flying by at full pelt. I never watch horse-racing on TV, as the experience does not come across at all; you have to be there. Having torn up our useless betting tickets, there would be a decent break before the next race. The entire area was filled with roulette wheels, wheels-of-fortune, and all the usual carnival attractions designed to part us from our cash. There was always a tiny chance of winning something in a raffle and we even sometimes did. Once I chose a replica rifle – really just a glorified 'cap gun' – as my prize. I had it for many years afterwards. This was our favourite part of race day, even though it had nothing whatsoever to do with horse-racing. I remember even paying for a picture signed in person right there by the legendary American frontiersman, 'Kit Carson'. The fact that the real Kit Carson had passed away about one hundred years previously was conveniently overlooked. Finally, it was time to get the bus back to Galway city and the train back to Gort. Dad would be there, ready to drive us home. They were some of the best days of my life, never to be forgotten.

Mam did not try to stop me from smoking, any more than Dad. On the contrary, she gave me money every day when I was going to secondary school, nominally to be spent on my 'lunch'. Considering she gave me my lunch as well, what was I supposed to do?

As well as baking bread almost every day, she would also bake large apple-tarts from time to time – though we always called it 'apple-cake'. She liked to use a lot of sugar. So much sugar, in fact, that it would melt or whatever the correct technical term is, and a river of hot syrup would run down inside the oven of the gas cooker and find its way on to the kitchen floor. The quick and easy solution to this crisis was to call in Lassie – our faithful dog – who would happily lick it all up, leaving the floor in pristine condition.

Home-made bread was fine but there was little that Mam enjoyed more than a fresh bakers' loaf from town. A loaf of bread usually came unsliced, and had a lovely dark brown crispy crust all across the top. Mam would seize the loaf in one hand, a breadknife in the other, and cut off the entire top crust, so that the giant slice was horizontal, not vertical. She would share almost everything with us, but in an understandable departure from her usual generosity, this was one speciality she steadfastly reserved for herself and herself alone. We were happy enough to make do with incomplete slices of bread, each one missing the top inch or so.

As I explained earlier, I never could learn prayers. Perhaps it would be more honest of me to admit that it was not just that I could not learn prayers, but that I was simply not prepared to put in the effort required to even try. This was an issue, not just at school, but at home as well. As in school, the worst experience of them all was the "rosary", a whole barrage of prayers stuck together, that my mother insisted on "giving out" (meaning to lead in prayer) every night. We were all expected to contribute to the "call and answer" system, and this was a major difficulty for me, considering I had never really learned any prayer off by heart, and was hugely disinterested in doing so. Every night, my heart sank when the rosary began. I immediately knew that my old companions, shame and misery, were now not far away. I dreaded the moment when Mam would call my name out, thus nominating me to recite the next dozen prayers or so. Admittedly, there was a lot of repetition involved, but that is of little use when you cannot complete even the simplest recital without stumbling over the words or simply coming to a sudden stop. Halted in mid-prayer, utterly frustrated and humiliated, I would go silent, expecting that my mother would surely take pity on me and move on to an alternative victim. After all, I had plenty sisters and brothers, all of whom appeared to have little difficulty with their prayers. She never did though, and just waited for me to get re-started, like an old battery that needs time to re-charge. And all this was going on while I was on my knees – talk about degradation. Eventually, I would have to get going again somehow, trying to quietly slur my way through the thing in a low enough tone of voice, so that nobody could really know for sure if I was saying the right words or not. These silent gaps could be quite lengthy at times, and I often wondered why my siblings did not lose patience and say "Oh, here, just let me do it". They never did. I shall have to have a talk with them about that, one of these days. Strangely, once the interminable thing was finished, there was never any further reference to it, or at least not until the entire debacle began again the following evening. It now occurs to me that the impasse might have been rather easily resolved by simply furnishing me with a written document containing the words of all the necessary prayers. I could read, after all. However, for all I know, there may well be a rule of the Catholic Church stating that prayers must be committed to memory and not just read from the page, since that would probably be too easy. Apparently, rather than flourish in this life, we were put here to suffer. In fact, one of the very few phrases I recall from my mother's recitation of the rosary is a reference to this world being likened to a "valley of tears". In any case the whole experience is like something that is branded in my soul. Sometimes at funerals, mourners will begin to recite the rosary. My preference is to quietly withdraw at that point, having nothing to contribute.

There is a place called Knock in County Mayo in the West of Ireland. It is best known now for its airport, but before that was built it was known as a "Marian shrine", meaning a place where there had been reports of miraculous apparitions of heavenly creatures. There are similar things in Lourdes in France and Fatima in Portugal. Back in the day, it was a regular thing for devout Catholics to go there on a pilgrimage. Once, when I was a small boy, I was informed that I was to be brought there with my mother and some neighbours. Having no real idea about what was involved, I looked forward to the day out with great eagerness, believing it might be something like the Galway Races or the Shanaglish Sports. As you may guess, I did not fully appreciate the nature of a pilgrimage. I soon found out though. The car journey - and it was a lengthy one - was an ordeal to begin with. The adults passed the time by saying the rosary, not just once but over and over. To make matters worse, an older boy who sat beside me in the rear of the car amused himself by physically tormenting me throughout the journey. When we finally arrived at Knock, there was nothing to do there, other than wander aimlessly about the place, reciting yet more prayers. The return journey was a tortuous replica of the outward one. Needless to say, I never returned to Knock, nor do I have any desire to do so.

Mam had one great over-riding fear in life – lightning. The approach of a thunderstorm would reduce this normally proud, confident woman to a quivering wreck. She would even go as far as getting into a wardrobe to escape the torture, even though she knew perfectly well that the flash of a lightning bolt is apparently so intense that it follows you pretty much everywhere. Dad would indulge himself in the age-old tradition of counting the number of seconds between the flash of lightning and the subsequent roll of thunder, deriving from the delay a rough indication of how far away the storm was from us at that point. Mam's mood was not helped at all when these calculations clearly showed that the epicentre of impending disaster was getting ominously closer and closer. The thing about this was that her extreme fear was contagious, to some degree. I would never admit it, of course, but I was scared too, especially when the storm was right in our immediate vicinity, and the sound of the thunder became less of a rumble and more of a savage explosive crack. As the epicentre passed and the storm began to move away, the relief was tremendous. It took me years to overcome that fear. As a matter of interest, there never was an actual lightning strike anywhere close to us. Now that I come to think of it, Mam also feared very high winds. On stormy days she always expected slates to fly off the roof of our house and decapitate somebody; of course it never happened. Whilst on a shopping trip to the town of Ennis on such a day, some of the very old roofs were indeed suffering under the onslaught of fierce winds, and Mam's subsequent description of it conjured up an image of slates flying about like snowflakes in a blizzard. The windiest day of all was September 16th, 1961 – that was the day Hurricane Debbie hit Ireland. I can still recall the tearing, screaming sound of a huge tree that was uprooted in the storm, crashing to the ground quite close to the house. It was just one of several large trees that came down and that we then used as playgrounds for years. We loved the storm, of course. We ran across the fields, amazed that we could lean right over into the wind that held us up like sails on a boat. I did not realise until I looked it up just now that 18 people were killed in Ireland on that day. It is still the most violent storm on record in this country.

Occasionally, Mam's ideas were less than optimal. One summer day, finding that a great deal of house-flies had accumulated on the inside of the windows, she had the apparently ingenious idea of sucking them all up with the vacuum cleaner. The plan worked well until she opened the device to empty the bag – while still in the house. Flies are hardy creatures; apparently they predate us by millions of years. The instant she opened the bag, all the flies re-emerged and headed straight back to the nearest window. On another unforgettable occasion, she decided for some reason best known to herself, to light a fire in a bedroom fireplace. It was a bit slow to take hold so she decided to add some 'fuel to the fire', as it were. In a temporary abandonment of basic common sense, she placed an old car tyre in the fireplace. This time the fire did get going, and with a vengeance, violently roaring up the chimney. To compound matters, the chimney was completely blocked at the top by an accumulation of crow's nests. The room quickly filled with thick black smoke that then began to spread out on to the landing and adjoining rooms. I was the only other person present and so I was quickly dispatched to fetch buckets of water. Apart from the pressure of repeatedly running upstairs carrying two buckets of water, knowing that if I was not fast and effective enough then the house was likely to burn down, the other major difficulty was actually locating the fireplace in a room full of thick, black, blinding rubber-derived smoke. Somehow, we managed to get it under control. She made me promise not to ever tell Dad – or anyone else - about the event. I have kept it to myself until now.

As I alluded to earlier, Mam was a member of the local branch of the ICA, the Irish Countrywomens Association. As in any other similar organisation, they held an AGM, at which the usual various roles were decided, such as chairperson, treasurer etc. On one such occasion, Mam informed us that she had been selected to be the branch's "National Representative". When we inquired as to the nature of the responsibilities associated with this particular role, she admitted that she had not made any specific inquiries in this regard. In fact, she further admitted that she was not quite sure if the term might actually have been "*In*ternational Representative". When she was departing the house to attend subsequent monthly meetings, we always politely inquired if the meeting were to be held in New York, Singapore, Timbuktoo or some other similar exotic location.

When I was quite young, Mam and Dad would sometime get dressed up and go out for the evening. We younger ones would be left in the care of our older siblings. When asked where they were going, which of course we routinely did ask, Mam always gave the same answer - she just said, "Off, off". I still don't know where they went, though I suppose it must have been to a dance or the cinema. I don't know where else there was to go.

Mam could be quite critical of all of us at times, and sometimes in a very direct manner, but equally she would become fiercely defensive if she felt that any member of the family was being slighted in any way. For example, once when Dad changed the car, a neighbouring woman unthinkingly remarked, "Sure it will be grand until you see your way to something better." Mam was enraged and resolved never to speak to the woman again. I think she kept that promise too – for a week at least.

My parents never took a holiday in their working lives. The endlessly repetitive nature of farm work meant the very concept of a vacation was practically out of the question. Indeed, I do not recall any local farmer ever taking a holiday. Very, very rarely, there would have been a requirement to attend a relative's wedding in what was then considered to be a far-away location such as Dublin. Mam and Dad would be missing for a couple of days, and the older members of the family, namely James and Anne, took on the mantle of responsibility. When this happened, I took great care to compile a carefully-written list of various tasks that I completed in their absence. These would typically be trivial matters such as ensuring that adequate quantities of firewood were available at all times. Of course, I knew perfectly well that they would never return empty-handed; there would always be "something from Dublin". My proudly presented list of jobs completed was never really checked, but it always felt safer to have it ready, just in case.

James

My brother James was about seven years older than me. In adult life that is nothing, but when I was a small boy, he came across as being practically indistinguishable from any fully-grown person. Also, he embellished this persona by acting in quite a serious manner. We attended primary school together for a little time - I was a member of the youngest cohort in the school, whilst he was one of the oldest. I can just barely remember him and his pal Joseph Callinan casually strolling around the place together; breaking into a run would have been an undignified concession for men of their stature. Smaller boys scattered at their approach; after all, this was James Brew and Joseph Callinan, not people to be trifled with. He went on to two years of secondary education at the Vocational School in Gort, and then attended boarding school at two agricultural colleges, spending a year in each. He once related to me how, when he was just a newly-arrived student in the agricultural college in Pallaskenry in County Limerick, he was instructed to go out and plough a field. Not only had he never previously ploughed, he had never even driven a tractor. Somehow, he managed. My sister Anne also attended boarding school in Castleconnell in County Limerick. These institutions were run by religious orders whose custom it was to keep their boarders on what was essentially a starvation diet. It was expected that parents would help out with food supplies or better still with hard cash that could be spent in the school "tuck shop", thus making ever greater contributions to the coffers of the order in question. I wasn't always much use at standing up for myself but one thing I had learned to insist upon, at the instigation of my older siblings; under no circumstances was I ever going to attend boarding school. In any case, by the time it was my turn, I think my parents could no longer afford it – lucky me.

Our parents had the best of intentions. They understood that education was the key to escaping the unrelenting cycle of unemployment and emigration that had held back the development of Irish society for so long. However, I believe that long periods in boarding school are not a good thing. Our family was effectively split up. Of course, most families are split up eventually, but this was happening at the age of twelve or thirteen, not at the age of eighteen or nineteen. Some of my older sisters and brothers almost became like strangers to me; strangers who showed up like some sort of exotic creatures at Christmas and other times for a few weeks, and then disappeared back into the "system". I believe they did their best to put a brave face on things, but, in reality, they may as well have been prisoners. Free secondary education had not yet been introduced, and so our parents must have really struggled to cover the payments. As usual, of course, I was completely and blissfully unaware of all this at the time, but I have no doubt my older siblings understood it well. I suppose they would have considered it churlish and ungrateful behaviour for them to have raised any objections to being sent to boarding school. For me, it took years to re-establish relationships with them – not until we were adults, really. And those missing years could never be recovered.

Long summer evenings were often spent playing in the large field just by the house. The public road ran by this field and sometimes, if passersby saw a game of football in progress, they would abandon their bicycles, hop over the wall and join in. Then, you could have everyone from the age of about five up to middle-aged men playing on the same pitch. One such evening, James and a neighbour, Tommy Cassidy, were playing in the field when they decided to go for a ramble in the uncultivated areas across the river. Reluctantly, I turned for home. "Do you not want to come with us?" they asked. I knew that I was too young to be allowed across the river, since there were so many dangers there for a small boy. "But it's alright when you're with us. We'll mind you" they assured me. So, I went with them, across the river for the first time. This was a major expedition for me. I'm sure we only covered a relatively small distance, but for me at the time, it might have been the Amazon rain forest, it all seemed so vast and unfamiliar. We came to a wide drain, which they could easily jump over, but where I would have no hope. I thought I would have to go back. But once again, James and Tommy saved the day. They stood on opposite sides of the drain and simply lifted and flung me across from one to the other, like a football. Talk about excitement. For them it was just another walk through, bog, crags and bushy areas. For me it was a whole new world. In later years I would often wander through that territory on my own, seeking out the most remote places. I would find a spot that was quite hard to get to, and then wonder had anybody ever stood on that exact location before. It is equally possible that nobody has stood in those exact spots ever since. Then there were some remote places that were fascinating simply because many people must have lived there in the distant past. The run-down remains of very old houses may still be found, sometimes where there is little or no arable ground, or indeed any visible clue as to how the occupants made a living. Also, very often there is no evidence of any road in or out of such places. How did those people exist?

My mother always made jam in the autumn; sometimes from apples, or maybe blackberries, or, our favourite, vegetable marrows. Vegetable marrow jam is so good it can only be described as marmalade's grown-up older sibling that you have never met before. To help keep James alive in boarding school, Mam decided to post some vegetable marrow jam to him. It was not a good idea. The glass jars cracked open in transit. When James opened up the consignment, he discovered shards of broken glass inextricably mixed through the jam. However, hunger is a strong motivating force, and so, he and some of his schoolmates invested a great deal of effort in separating jam and glass fragments.

In between stints at agricultural college, James worked hard at home on the farm. He was rarely idle. You could often see him carrying a huge haul of hay on his back to be fed to cattle. I had little interest in farm work so I could not honestly say where exactly he was bringing the hay from or, indeed, where he was bringing it to. We smaller ones were a bit wary of him and his serious ways, so, generally gave him a wide berth. Once, and only once, I deliberately provoked him. He was up a ladder that was laid against a big apple-tree and he was carefully picking bags of cooking apples to be set aside for the winter. Like I say, he was rarely idle. The apples grew in great abundance in the orchard near our house and they needed to be carefully handpicked so as not to be damaged. Walking by, in an idle moment, a sudden temporary madness came over me. Locating a good-sized stick, I flung it with some force up towards the area of the tree close to where James was working, knocking a great bunch of apples to the ground, and in the process, ruining them. He was furious. He came down the ladder rather quickly, and realising I was in trouble, I ran for it. He came after me. I was a fast runner though and reckoned I had a good chance of outpacing him. I easily cleared the wall between the orchard and the haggard in one fine leap. Across the haggard, I still held a good lead. "Keep going", I told myself, "He'll get tired and go back to his apple-tree". But I had miscalculated. The stone wall at the far side of the haggard was both wide and high. There was no escape. He caught me, and for the only time in my life, I was beaten on the backside. I know all forms of corporal punishment are essentially wrong, but, even so, I surely deserved it.

Before chainsaws became affordable and thus more commonplace, a 'cross-cut' saw would sometimes be deployed. This was a large two-man saw with a handle at each end. Working a saw like this is sheer hard labour, and it is another memory I have of James and his relentless work ethic; him and our Dad cutting down a large tree with the use of a crosscut saw. A new cowshed, or 'cowhouse' as we always called it, was constructed over a period of time, with much of the work done by Dad himself. We all thought we were helping out, but I think mostly we just got in the way. James was different though – he worked hard at it from time to time. I clearly recall spending time with him late one evening as he finished off part of the concrete floor by the light of a rather weak oil lamp, there being no electricity in the still only partly-constructed building at the time. Later on, Dad undertook construction of another farm building; a new pigsty, or 'piggery', as we called it. When it was about half-built, there was a sort of scaffolding along the rear wall with a walkway the length of the building. It was really quite a small pigsty but it looked huge to me at the time. One day while Dad was away, James was left in charge of 'construction', such as it was. He was serious about his work, and also about his play. When he had finished whatever job had been entrusted to him, he spent the rest of the afternoon marching over and back along the length of the suspended walkway, a length of wood posing as a rifle in his hands, as though he were on guard duty, protecting the premises from attack. In time, he signed up to the part-time activities of the FCA; a sort of territorial army of reservists. They gave him a uniform and a real rifle which he kept in the wardrobe of his bedroom. Now that I come to think of it, there were always guns around the place. That sort of thing is simply not allowed any more.

When James finished Primary school, Mam and Dad were determined that he would go on to Secondary school; not a given at that time, by any means. St. Flannans in Ennis, an eminent establishment, was where they wanted him to go, and to this end, they arranged for him to attempt the entrance scholarship exam. James had other ideas though; he did not want to go to Flannans, and so he did something that was really very much outside his normal behavioural system. Knowing that our parents could not afford the fees for Flannans, thus rendering his likely attendance there entirely dependent on a really good result from the scholarship examination, he did the only thing he felt he could do in the circumstances; he deliberately flunked the exam. He wanted to attend Gort Vocational School (known colloquially as "the Tech"), where he wished to immerse himself in what he considered to be more practical activities such as woodwork and metalwork. And so that is where he went. The peculiar thing about his decision-making in this instance is that while he was certainly well able to perform useful manual work, the truth is that he was probably much better with his head than he ever was with his hands. Later on, in his twenties, when he was employed by the Department of Agriculture, he realised that not having a full secondary education, and not having had the opportunity to sit the Leaving Certificate examination could be a drag on his career advancement, he took it upon himself to study for and complete the Leaving Cert as a mature student.

I remember James and Anne having discussions about serious matters such as politics, the economy and so on. I had no idea what they were on about, but was fascinated just the same. I heard them use terms like "production", "service industries" and the like. I was convinced that I would never reach this impossibly high level of conversational ability. In his twenties, James prided himself on being able to complete the famous Irish Times cryptic Derek Crozier 'Crosaire' crossword in less than an hour. I was middle-aged before I managed to do it at all, and certainly not in an hour. When I was a teenager and explained to James that I had lost all belief in any form of religion, he asked me what I did believe in. "Nothing", I told him. "Oh, well then", he said, "That makes you a nihilist". It felt good to be told you were something distinctive.

It is a rare thing now to see a young man smoking a pipe. Indeed it has become a very rare thing to see anyone smoking a pipe – young or old, male or female. James smoked a pipe for some years, in his twenties and early thirties. He was an unassuming individual, and certainly was entirely unaffected by the various fashion trends of the day. But I always harboured an unspoken suspicion that pipe-smoking was something of an affectation for him, perhaps an attempt to project a more serious persona – as if he did not already appear serious enough. I suppose he became addicted in time. In any case, the arrival of Alice in his life more or less coincided with the demise of the pipe.

When James left home in the mid-sixties and took up employment with the Department of Agriculture in Sligo, and later in Dublin, he would arrive home for the occasional weekend. He acquired his first car, a second-hand black Volkswagen Beetle. I can still remember the registration number – it was CIE 653. In fact, he had a series of such cars, always a Beetle, and always black. Coming home from school, it was always exciting for me to see the familiar shape of the black Beetle parked outside the house – big brother was home. Arriving in to the house bearing a couple of packets of biscuits for Mam, he would immediately be greeted with her regular inquiry; "James, did you bring those biscuits from Sligo?" It was important to her that the gift was as exotic as possible, and in that time even Sligo seemed like a rather remote location. James had probably got the biscuits at any old shop along the way, but he would never tell her. Being essentially a pragmatic and rational character, or at least wishing to be perceived as such, he would reply, "Sure, what does it matter? All the biscuits come from the Jacobs factory in Dublin anyway."

Between the time when he finished agricultural college and before he took up employment as an Agricultural Officer, James spent a period of time working at home on the farm, perhaps for a year or so, I don't quite remember how long it was. What I do remember is that the only real 'down-time' that he enjoyed was to travel to a dance at the weekend in one of the local towns, usually Ennis or Gort. This was the 1960's, a time when showbands and dancehalls were enjoying a huge boom. Having no real money of his own, James was entirely dependent on my parents to ensure that he had enough cash in his pocket for a Sunday night out. I vividly recall one such Sunday evening, after a fine summer day, when Mam, Dad, James and I were the only members of the family that happened to be present. I was a young teenager, James an 'old' one. As usual, he needed cash for the evening, but, as luck would have it, our parents simply did not have it in hand. Cash was king; there were no ATM's, no credit or debit cards, and something like Revolut on a hand-held device would not even have been considered in the most extravagant imaginings of a science fiction writer. James had worked hard all week, as he always did, looking forward, I am sure, to the only break that he ever really expected to get, namely the Sunday night dance. I distinctly remember the feeling of being humiliated for him, even though I was merely a witness to his disappointment. Had he thrown a fit, freaked out, cursed his parents or whatever, I think it might have been entirely understandable. But that was not James' style. It was obvious that he was devastated, but he took it like the man that he already was. He just said something along the lines of "Oh, alright so," and he went into the parlour, a little-used 'front room', from where you could presently hear the sound of him playing the tin whistle. He was never a great player, but like everything else he attempted, he tried his best. I could not see him but I knew exactly where he was and how he looked. He would be sitting at one end of the large oval table, perched on the table itself, with one foot planted firmly on the floor and the other leg swinging back and forth in time to the music.

James passed away in 2007.

James and Anne

Anne

An adventure involving Anne occurred on a fine day in summer. Dad and some of the others were working at building a large haycock over in the 'four acre' field. I was still too small for this kind of work. My mother had just left for Ennis on her bicycle. She was barely out of sight when Anne decided that now would be a good time to fulfil what must have been a long-held ambition - to drive the family car. She was about eleven or twelve years old.

In those times, car theft was virtually unheard of, and so the keys were never taken out of the ignition. So that was handy. She got it started alright and also managed to get it into gear. In fairness, she must have been quite observant, because she had clearly grasped a good deal of the basics. Not enough, though – like steering, for example. The car took off and immediately turned to the right and headed downhill. She somehow stopped it and jumped out. I could see that things were seriously out of control, and I was so scared, I clambered for safety up on to the seat of an old horse-drawn mowing machine that stood in the yard for years. James appeared from somewhere, and I still have a mental image of him manfully putting his weight to the front of the car, hopelessly attempting to push it back up to where it came from. He would always try to save her skin – and often did. However, he had to give way as the car began to slowly move again, sliding inexorably down the slope until it eventually buried its nose in the wall with a crunching sound.

Just in case Anne would be tempted to try reversing back up the slope, James took the keys out of the ignition (I had not realised you could even do that), and took them over the field to be handed to Dad.

Perhaps the lesson stood to her as she became a good driver some thirty-odd years later.

Years later while she was employed by CIE in the railway station, Anne stayed in 'digs' in Ennis. The six-day working week was still the norm in the sixties, so she would arrive home for what was left of the 'weekend' on a Saturday evening. She never came empty-handed. Money was no obstacle, as Anne always spent more than she could afford. She closely followed this financial model throughout her entire life.

Supermarkets had arrived and with them, strange, exotic foods. Well, strange and exotic to us, anyway. Like curry, and coffee, both of which I tasted for the first time – and hated.

It was bonanza time as she brought home books, magazines and records.

The buying spree culminated in the purchase of a Garelli moped. The first time she came home on it, I took it for a spin over the road and immediately I was the first to crash it. I desperately hoped the scratches on the paintwork would not be noticed, and I believe I got away with it. Some years later, I would use the same moped myself to travel to and from secondary school. I believe I was the very first student to use a form of mechanised personal transport for this purpose in the town of Gort.

The usual practice on Sunday was that Anne would commandeer the kitchen table for the afternoon, and construct a dress for the Sunday night dance. I paid little attention to this procedure at the time, but it is a mystery to me now how an article of clothing could be put together in such a short time. While that was going on I would sometimes be dispatched to a neighbour's house, usually the Ryans, to find out if they were planning to go to a dance that night (they always were), and if Anne could travel with them.

I remember the very occasion when Anne got me started smoking. She was an 'old' teenager, I was a 'young' one and we were on a train travelling to Dublin. She needed to go to there for something, I don't recall exactly what, and brought me along for company, I suppose. We were reading the usual rubbish magazines stocked at railway stations, when she whipped out a pack of cigarettes and lit up. She wasn't really a smoker, but in the sixties pretty much everyone smoked – it was almost obligatory. Suddenly she thrust the pack of cigarettes right under my nose. I had never smoked and my hesitation must have showed, because she said;

"Well, you do smoke, don't you?"

Not wanting to appear uncool, I, of course, replied;

"Oh yeah, yeah", and I took it. Had I but known that about ten years later I would be desperately trying to smoke my last cigarette.

I was really shocked at how unpleasant the whole experience turned out to be. When you don't know how to smoke properly, it goes in all the wrong places – up your nose, in your eyes etc. It's even worse when you finally figure out how to suck it into your lungs. And all this time you are trying to maintain an air of casual enjoyment. I wonder now if she was keeping up the same pretence as I was. It's tough to be a teenager.

The Kodak Instamatic camera was a sixties design classic. Released in 1963, it brought easy and affordable colour photography to the masses for the first time. Anne got one, of course, because she had to get everything new that came out, regardless of whether she could afford it or not. We have her to thank for the hilarious pictures that we still have of those '60's Christmasses in our house.

Dad used to be a member of a local group that entered quiz competitions, and in time, Anne and James were pressed into service also. I knew I could never match their apparent genius in such matters. In my teens I, in turn, was requested to participate, but I declined, knowing that I knew nothing and that I had no desire for such ignorance to be publicly exposed. Later on, in my twenties, I did take part in a quiz along with my Dad and some others. To my amazement, we won, and I received the only trophy I ever got in my life. I still remember the question that clinched victory for us. They played a short snatch of a song which I correctly identified as 'That's Life' by Frank Sinatra. I was never a Sinatra fan, but I was grateful to be at least a little bit familiar with his music just that one time.

In the late sixties, when Anne lived in London, I occasionally wrote letters to her. I did not know it, of course, but she kept some of those letters. After she passed away in 2014, amongst her correspondence I discovered some of the letters that I had written to her almost half a century earlier.

Local Characters

Mattie

Mattie was a local farmer who lived on his own. His wife and family had long since left him, unable to tolerate his miserly ways. Much of the time, you would see Mattie wearing a heavy overcoat, but in the traditional way, that is with a length of rope around his waist, where one would normally expect to see a belt. He always had a grizzled, unshaven appearance, yet never grew a full beard. He had patches of land in various nearby locations, and seemed to spend a great deal of his time walking herds of cattle from one place to the other. As he passed by our house, he would often drop in for a chat. My mother would offer tea, of course, and he would always accept, even if in a half-grudging sort of way, saying something along the lines of, "Except a small sup". Even when she fed him well, a thing she sometimes did, on the way out he might say, "Well, that'll keep me going until I get a square meal". Perhaps all that makes him sound like a really bad man, which I don't think he really was, just not very well-mannered, and also of course, extremely miserly. It was well-known that he lived a very primitive existence. The house had apparently never been cleaned since his family had left him. It was said that when he ate, he simply laid a fresh sheet of newspaper on the table each time, never wiping down the surface, and placing each subsequent sheet of paper on top of all the previous ones that already lay there. It was also said that he cooked a joint of meat simply by laying it right on to the open fire, peeling off and eating the cooked outer shell, and then putting the rest back on the fire again for the next time. And it was said that he regularly bathed; that is if you count once a year in the sea at Lahinch as regular. As a young lad, my brother James once did some work for

Mattie, helping him to weed a field of carrots. When a call of nature comes to one in such a place, it is customary to go at least as far as the headland to take care of things. (The headland is the thin strip of unploughed ground around the perimeter of a cultivated field). Mattie, though, simply relieved himself right in the middle of the field, over his own carrots. James made a mental note that we were not to accept any of Mattie's vegetables when they were harvested, and even if he insisted on giving us any, which was unlikely, we were definitely not going to eat them.

One of the few things that Mattie was prepared to pay for was the Sunday paper, in this case, The Sunday Press, the same paper that we also took. Mattie himself rarely travelled to the shops, since he was so disinclined to spend any money, and so there was an arrangement whereby we took his copy of the Sunday paper as well as our own, and we held it until such time as he called to collect it. Sometimes it might almost be time for the next edition by the time he did collect it. We were not allowed to read or even touch Mattie's copy. If Mam as much as saw you attempt to pick it up, she would say, "Oh, don't touch that paper, that's Mattie's." Fascinated by newspapers from a very young age, once, I sneaked a look at Mattie's Sunday Press. I was probably just about able to read at this stage. I was amazed to see that it was exactly the same as our own. There was so much care taken with keeping Mattie's paper untouched and in pristine condition, I had naturally assumed that everyone's copy was an individual production, custom made, as it were. I suppose it was my first introduction to the world of mass production.

A large golden-coloured dog lay outside our school door every day. His name was Prince; he was fed and generally looked after by our teacher. But he was not her dog. He was Mattie's dog. Every farmer had a dog for rounding up cattle and sheep. Clearly, Prince understood where he was being fed and cared for, so he lived a great part of his life in the schoolyard. However, he had dual loyalties, and when Mattie needed him for his regular cattle-moving activities, he came looking for him and Prince obediently answered the call. Everyone gave their dog a name, of course, but Mattie was unaware that his had even been christened by somebody else. Giving a dog a name, either a good or a bad one, would not have been something that rated very highly on Mattie's list of priorities. When canine assistance was needed, Mattie came and stood on the road outside the school, which was just a few hundred yards from his house, calling out, "The dog, the dog, the dog", until Prince emerged and joined him.

Mattie managed to break one of his legs in a farm accident, but nobody knew exactly how it had occurred. The story was put about that he sat on a branch of a tree while sawing through the part of the same branch closer to the main trunk, thus leading to the inevitable result. We never believed it; Mattie was a terribly unsophisticated man, but he was certainly not stupid. When my mother, who liked to have the real facts about every situation at her disposal, asked him directly what had happened, he would only reply, "Ah, sure 'twas the mi-adh". Mi-adh is the Irish word for misfortune.

I don't know how Mattie came by the name "King", but that was how many local people referred to him. My mother would not allow us to use that nickname, apparently believing that it was a sarcastic belittling of the man; which it probably was.

As well as claiming ownership of a dog that he did not care for, Mattie also had a working horse, as many farmers still did, even though tractors were largely taking over their functions. One day as Mattie passed by our school at playtime, accompanied by both the dog and the horse, my brother Francis, never one to pass up an opportunity for a pithy comment, called out, "Oh, look, there goes the King, the Prince and the mare."

Though Mattie had always been a regular caller to our house, his visits had always been more in the nature of a traditional neighbourly catch-up call, rather than one based on any kind of personal relationship. Like many old men who lived alone in the West of Ireland, it seemed that he was not really capable of maintaining a meaningful relationship. As old age advanced upon him, Mattie began to lose his sight. I happened to be there for one of his final visits to our house. He could just about find his way around familiar places, but as he turned to leave our kitchen, he fumbled with the door, and found himself facing into the corner of the room, unable to see his way out. Certainly, he would have been regarded as a flawed individual, and he had never been a really close friend to our family, or a fun guy to be around. Even so, it was sad to see someone who had been so independent reduced to having to be guided along by one of us, just to find his way out of our house and set on the road home.

Christy

When Mattie died, his son Christy, already a middle-aged man, took the place over. Christy had inherited not just the farm, but also his father's attitude to money, and that is to say, he rarely spent any. He was extremely hard-working, already running another farm that he had elsewhere, as well as holding down a fulltime job. This left little time for leisure activities, and that was fine with Christy, for leisure was not something that featured greatly in his life. The only "down-time" activity that he took time out for was to talk. He loved to talk. Part of the land that he now owned bordered ours, and on summer evenings, we sometimes encountered each other on the road and chatted for a while. I was a teenager by then, so spent a good deal of my time just sauntering about, as teenagers do. Christy knew that I took an interest in current affairs, and since he was not prepared to rise to the cost of having a radio fitted in his car, nor, I suppose, even in his house, he would ask me about the news of the day. His one abiding passion was his strong interest in the concept of militant republicanism. In the late sixties and early seventies, the chaos in Northern Ireland was at its worst, with fresh atrocities reported almost every day. In the normal course of events, if a life like Christy's could ever be described as normal, he seemed like a relatively civilised, not-too-badly-adjusted individual, but when it came to discussing the presence of British soldiers on what he regarded as Irish territory, he assumed another persona altogether. If I related that there had been an IRA attack, in which soldiers had been killed, he was elated. The more of them that were killed, the better he liked it. When I reported such gruesome events, he might comment, "Oh, I'm glad I met you now. That's great news altogether". He even named his two dogs in honour of a politician named Kevin Boland, who, around that time, had just founded a new republican-leaning party called Aontacht Eireann. He called the dogs Boland and Aontacht.

Christy did not smoke or drink, was unmarried and since he had no social life whatsoever, it was extremely unlikely that he would ever meet a partner. I doubt very much that he had ever been to a bar or restaurant. Apparently, his colleagues in the place where he was employed regularly tried to persuade him to meet up for an evening out, but without success. Once, he admitted that some of them had played a nasty trick on him. They had eventually worn him down, persuading him to meet them for an evening's entertainment, and, just this once, Christy finally relented and agreed to do so. They named the venue, the date and the time. But when Christy arrived there on the appointed evening, he found that the place had been closed for years. It would never happen again.

Christy was very thin and slightly built, almost to the point of emaciation. That was not surprising considering that he worked himself to the bone every day from morning till night, not allowing himself the slightest indulgence. He died well before his time, leaving his wealth behind him. It would seem that all his hard work had been for nothing.

Willie Grady

Willie Grady, an old man, lived almost directly across the road from Moyrhee school. Two pear trees grew in the field right by the gable end of his small thatched house. Willie guarded his pears as best he could, but he was up against it. It was impossible for us to resist the challenge of sneaking in over the wall, climbing the trees and stealing pears, usually before they were even ripe enough to eat. If Willie spotted us, we feared there could be trouble, though I believe he was really a harmless old fellow. Whatever pears survived our raiding parties were harvested by Willie and these he stored in biscuit tins in his kitchen. The irony was that if you went in to Willie and asked him, he would readily take the juiciest pear from a biscuit tin and simply hand it over. If you were entirely without moral scruples, the trees could be raided even more easily on a Friday afternoon, since this was the time when everyone aged 70 or older repaired to the post office, some miles away, to collect their weekly pension. My sister Anne pushed Willie to the limit one day. He spotted her already well up the pear tree. "Come down out of there, Anne Brew", he shouted, "I can see you". We all knew that Willie had one glass eye, having lost an eye many years before in a shooting accident on our own land. Also, Anne had little respect for her elders. “How can you see me, if you only have one eye?” she shouted back, continuing to concentrate on her pear-stealing activities. The other abiding memory I have of Willie is the wonderful display of colourful tulips that grew every year in the relatively small garden space in front of his neat little house. When Willie passed away and a new owner took the place over, not only was his house bulldozed out of existence, but so also were his pear trees and, of course, his display of tulips. I have never forgotten them. In the springtime, I find there is little that lifts the heart more than a colourful display of tulips.

Travelling People

While it is true to say that most people in the countryside were not particularly well off, nevertheless, with few exceptions, most got by with at least a reasonable standard of living. And there was certainly no real shortage of food; after all, most farmers produced their own meat, vegetables, grain and dairy products. But there existed in society a sort of underclass that generally survived on the edge of ruin; these were the travelling people. Most people referred to them by the name ‘tinkers’, simply because the trade of tinsmith had been their way of life for a long time, repairing leaky buckets and other containers for the farming community. The arrival of better quality aluminium buckets, and especially plastic containers, really put paid to the ‘tinker’s trade’. From being poor, they went to being really poor.

But even within their own society, there were different strata to be observed. Some travelled with a degree of comfort and style in well-turned-out horse-drawn caravans. They appeared to be closer to the top of the food chain, if such a crude term may be used. I clearly recall when one such group moved on, following a lengthy stay nearby, we discovered they had left behind masses of necklaces made of large gaily-coloured beads. Initially, my sisters thought that all their dreams had come true – an almost endless source of free jewellery; what more could any young woman want? But I don't remember that they ever wore any of it; apparently, it was just not fashionable. I suppose if we had held on to the stuff, changes in the fashion industry might have brought us untold wealth - who knows?

The much poorer travelling families merely owned a pony or two and camped on the side of the road in rough tents that appeared unbelievably wretched to our eyes, and must have been especially so in cold and wet conditions. It was no surprise to learn that their life expectancy fell very far short of the national average. How they could survive in such dire circumstances is almost beyond imagining now. Having said that, we grew to take their occasional local presence for granted, and with a child's acceptance for the world being the way that it is, regardless of how grotesque that may be, I have to admit that we generally did not pay a great deal of attention to them. My mother was something of an exception in this regard. When the women - and it was always the women, and they always wore a shawl - came to the house with their most common request, namely asking for food and milk for their child, Mam would give them what they needed, but also engage them in conversation. In this way, she came to know many of the families quite well, over the years. A common remark from these women, some of them quite young, was that their husband had passed away. Whenever Mam asked one of these ladies about the cause of her husband's death, the answer was always the same; "Twas the heart, ma'am." In later years, when many travelling families moved to settle in the urban environment, Mam would still encounter these women in the local town of Ennis, and they remembered her, stopping for a chat and to catch up. In time, though, the age-old connection between the travellers and the farming community, such as it was, gradually diminished, until, eventually, it petered out altogether.

As a child, I could not but observe one of the interesting social protocols of the time. Unlike almost any other casual visitor, who would certainly be invited in and offered tea, no member of the travelling community who came to the door would ever venture past the threshold, nor indeed would any of them ever be invited to do so. Apparently, it was one thing to provide charity to them, in the way of essential food supplies and so on, but the lines along which social boundaries were drawn, were clearly understood by all, and never transgressed.

Many times, as we walked or cycled past these road-side encampments, the men would call out to us. The women and children never did. I was always fascinated by their favourite question; "What time is it?" I failed to understand what relevance the time of day held for someone whose daily existence appeared very unlikely to be dotted with any type of urgent appointments. In any case, it was useless to ask us, since most of us did not possess anything as exotic as a wristwatch, or any other type of jewellery for that matter. I felt it was somewhat rude not to help out, though, so I often just guessed what the time might roughly be, and passed my wisdom on, replying, for example; "I'd say it could be about two o'clock."

Nuts and eggs

My mother reared hens, and since they produced far more eggs than we could eat, she often sold the excess to various shops, both locally and in town. Another "get-rich-quick" scheme that we youngsters engaged in was to pick hazelnuts in the autumn. These grew in great abundance all over the nearby crags. It took a lot of time and patience to collect even a reasonable-sized sack of them. I can still just barely recall the first time that my older sisters and brothers allowed me to accompany them on one of these outings, picking hazelnuts in a nearby crag. We moved from hazel bush to hazel bush, stripping each one of 'ripe' nuts, i.e. the ones that were nice and brown-looking. As the autumn evening grew darker, I could barely make out where my siblings were located. I remember a feeling of panic coming over me, as I feared that they might depart for home without me, and I would be left wandering all night in what looked to me like a vast forest of hazel. I also remember not wanting to call out to them, as I felt that might leave me open to derision. Why was I so timid? I don't know, but it was a timidity that stunted much of the enjoyment of my early life and teenage years.

There was more to picking hazelnuts than simply taking them from the bush. You had to individually remove every nut from the surrounding green husk. There was no time for this in the actual 'picking' session, so it was left to be done later at home. This reduced your large sack of hazelnuts to something much smaller. Our parents would then bring these with them on their next trip to town, to be sold, on our behalf, to various greengrocers. After days of work we would probably end up with just a few shillings. It wasn't really worth it but I still did it anyway. It was something to do.

A local chap, a bit older than we were, was occasionally sent by his mother to buy eggs from us. He was not one of our more welcome visitors, as he was not a very likable fellow and so my mother would not really encourage him to stay and have tea, the standard procedure with all visitors. But he liked to make himself welcome anyway, settling himself comfortably in his favourite chair, tilting it on its rear legs and leaning back against the wall. I can picture him still - and it is not a pretty picture. He arrived one day while I was in the process of removing the hazelnuts from the husks. Without invitation, he proceeded to help himself to fistfuls of my hard-earned hazelnuts, cracking them with his teeth and dropping the broken shells all around him on the kitchen floor. I resented his behaviour, but worse was to follow. When it came to paying my mother for the eggs, rather than simply hand over the cash, he was in the habit of flinging the coins on to the kitchen floor, some of them rolling in under the large dresser, from where it was practically impossible to recover them. My mother was disgusted by his objectionable behaviour, but there was not a great deal that she could do about it; his mother held a position of some authority in the community and so the family were untouchable.

The politician

T.D.'s, our parliamentary representatives were, in general I think, more highly regarded in those days than they are now. Some even had loyal followers, almost like rock stars of later times. Despite the widely-held suspicion of socialism, or anything that could even be remotely connected with Communism, or the hated Russians, my mother was a great admirer of the socialist politician, Noel Browne. But then, practically all Irish women were big fans of his, and, no surprise, for he was just about the only politician of his time who actively stood up for women's rights. He probably could have been elected in any constituency with women's votes alone. Another politician she had a lot of time for was Dr. Paddy Hillery. He was a local T.D. for the Clare constituency for many years, as well as a cabinet minister, and later, was to become President of Ireland. She could pick them alright. When she felt our rights were being overlooked in some way, or that the family could do with the benefit of intercession by a parliamentary representative with clout at the highest table, she would say, "I'm going to write off to Dr. Hillery about it". I don't know if she ever wrote any of those letters.

If she did and only posted one tenth of them, Paddy Hillery would have needed extra secretarial staff just to deal with Mam's requests alone. Years later, I was on a flight from Shannon to somewhere in Europe, I have forgotten exactly where. I happened to be seated right beside Dr. Hillery, who by then was Ireland's first European Commissioner. He appeared to be extremely busy with stacks of papers spread all around him. Not a solitary word of conversation passed between us; not as much as a hello. Had Mam been there, the work of the European Commission would have had to be put on the back-burner.

Paddy Burnell and Paddy O'Brien

Paddy Burnell lived in the house nearest to us, a small cottage situated on high ground and with a view stretching all the way to the Burren mountains; a magnificent view that we took for granted as we passed by, but one that I now realise many people would almost die for. The cottage was Paddy's home, but at the time he shared it with an old man called Paddy O'Brien. To us, Paddy O'Brien looked like some kind of strange and amazing being simply because he had an extremely long grey beard. Beards were almost unheard of then, but Paddy's looked like he had never shaved in his life. And, quite possibly, he never had. How he came to be living there I do not know; his original family home was a couple of miles away. For the generation that preceded ours, it was not that unusual for some people to move to and live in other people's houses. Some large families, for example, would 'offload' a child to a household of relatives, where there was a smaller number of children or perhaps none at all. It was a rather crude version of social redistribution, I suppose, though if anyone had dared say that in holy, Catholic Ireland, then it would have been banned immediately. When I was still very young, maybe still pre-school, my sister Gerita and I had got into the habit of crossing the fields and visiting various neighbours for no particular reason. I recall when we visited the two Paddys unannounced one day. They made us welcome, and both played musical instruments for our entertainment. Paddy Burnell played the concertina, and I do not exactly recall what Paddy O'Brien played but it may have been the fiddle. It was a concert with two players for an audience of two.

In later years the two Paddys were split up, when Paddy O'Brien moved on to live in another neighbour's house. That sort of thing was not so unusual. Paddy Burnell was not left on his own for very long, when a fellow called Mick Hynes moved in. Mick tended to boss Paddy around, and we knew that he sent Paddy into our place to dig potatoes and vegetables from our garden. When you know your garden, the evidence that somebody has been pilfering your crops is perfectly obvious, and we had no doubt about who was really behind it. We never confronted them, since there were acres of the stuff, and so it was small fry really. The funny thing about it was that if they had simply asked right out, they would have been invited to help themselves anyway.

Paddy was a simple man. Once, he burst into our house in the middle of the day and blurted out to my mother,

"Oh, isn't it terrible about Mrs. Kennedy?"

My mother had no idea to what he was referring and so she invited him to elaborate. He explained that Mrs. Kennedy had just had a heart attack.

"Oh, the poor woman, that's terrible. I hope she'll be alright." Mam replied. Then she began to think. There was no family called Kennedy in the parish, nor indeed anywhere for miles around.

"And what Mrs. Kennedy is that anyway Paddy?" she asked.

"Mrs. Kennedy from the Kennedys of Castleross", he answered.

The Kennedys of Castleross was a popular daily radio drama.

The Ryans

The Ryan family lived over the road from us, at the end of a long narrow road or boreen that went up over a hill before descending again to the house. On each side of the boreen high banks rose well above our heads, with some trees rising above that again, almost giving the effect of a tunnel. In the summer thousands of wild strawberries grew on those banks. You could spend hours in a place like that, munching away. Sadly, it has all since been bulldozed away. This was another house that Gerita and I would call to, out of the blue. The household consisted of the old man, Patty, and his grown-up offspring, namely his two sons Patrick and Jimmy and his daughter Mary. Mary Ryan was always very nice to us, but one particular visit went badly wrong, mostly down to faulty judgement on my part. We had climbed onto the hay piled up in the Ryan's hay-barn, a place we were not really supposed to go. To us, it seemed like we were on a skyscraper. We could see old Patty Ryan far below and we thought it was really funny to see him from that point of view, cap first, as it were. He heard our laughter, spotted us high up on the hay, and delivered a stern lecture, insisting that we come down immediately. Feeling that we were rather safe perched up there, and that he could not get to us, as he was far too old, we stood our ground. I even went as far as to call him names. I had recently picked up the phrase "monkey-faced eejit" from my Dad, who liked to use such terms in jest. So I let Patty have it. "We're not coming down, you monkey-faced eejit", I shouted down to him. He was outraged, of course, and eventually we had to come down and face the music. We slunk away up the boreen in tears. I can still recall Mary running out especially to wave goodbye. She had already forgiven us for insulting her father. We did not go back there for a while, but whenever my brother Francis visited, old man Ryan would question him with great suspicion. "Wasn't it you that called me a monkey-faced eejit?" "Oh, no, that was Johnny." "I don't know. I'm thinking it was you," and so on.

The Ryans had an electric kettle, a thing that was still pretty unusual, almost a luxury. In the early days of electrification in Ireland, back in the thirties, apparently it was mostly used just to provide light, and so many people referred to electricity as simply "the light". When Patty Ryan first saw the electric kettle being used to boil water, he is said to have remarked, "Isn't it marvellous all the same, you can boil the water off the light". And now, of course, producing electricity from light has actually become a real thing. Even though the Ryans had a gas cooker in their kitchen, as did we, Mary still baked bread every day on an open fire in the big traditional hearth. I found it fascinating to watch this old-fashioned process, with the bread in a covered heavy iron pan, which I believe is called a skillet. She would settle it on the hot coals, and then cover it with even more hot coals. It was probably the last local house in which cooking was carried out in this manner.

In later years, when I was in primary school and when Patty Ryan had passed away, and so the coast was safely clear for me, I called to the house every month to deliver a religious magazine called "The Far East". I had no fondness for religious publications; it was a job I was given and also I liked visiting neighbours, especially the ones who were nice to me. The Far East was published by a missionary order. I voraciously consumed all forms of reading matter, but, like pretty much all religious magazines, and there were several, The Far East was extremely boring, except for the children's corner. This featured a regular column, supposedly written by a schoolboy called Pudsy Ryan, who could not spell. The joke was always the same; that is, a series of wrongly spelled words and poorly constructed sentences. Once you had seen it a couple of times, it was not that funny anymore. But we always read it anyway. In later years, the pop group Slade made a good career from writing their lyrics in a similar fashion, such as "Mama Weer All Crazee Now". Perhaps they had been reading The Far East.

Mary and Joe O'Connor

I also delivered The Far East to another neighbouring woman, Mary O'Connor. A really kind lady, she lived at the end of an even much, much longer narrow boreen, in a house that was situated so remarkably close to the river, it always amazed me that the water did not actually wash in the front door, especially when the flood was high after heavy rain in the winter time. In the springtime, daffodils grew there. Mary shared the house with her brother Joe, and Paddy O'Brien. Yes, the same bearded old Paddy O'Brien who had previously played music for Gerita and me in Paddy Burnell's house next door to us. Mysteriously, he had moved again. Mary and Joe were about the same age as my Dad, and they had all been schoolmates many years before. He and Dad were the first two in the locality to get a car, ours having arrived the same year as I did, 1952. It was already quite an elderly vehicle, a 1936 'Baby' Ford. We had it for years, and I can recall travelling in it, particularly because there was a small hole in the floor, through which you could see the road passing beneath you. Its number plate began with the letters ID, meaning it had originally been registered in County Cavan. Cavan seemed so far away from us, it may as well have been Fiji. One of those old number plates survived around the place for years, long after the car had been scrapped. By 2036 it would have been a century old, and I suppose it would be of some value, at least sentimental. We should have kept it. Joe O'Connor was also one of the first to acquire a tractor, and he could be hired to do agricultural contracting work such as ploughing and so on. Once, while he was mowing hay for us, I stood nearby, always fascinated by machinery. Completely unknown to us, a turkey from my mother's flock had taken to the meadow to lay her eggs. Even the noise of the approaching machinery was not enough to persuade her to abandon her clutch of eggs, and so her legs were cut off by the blade of the mower. Joe, a phlegmatic individual, was well accustomed to the blood and guts nature of country life. He simply placed the bleeding bird into my hands and told me to take it home to my mother, which I did. I only had to cross one other field to get home but it felt like one of the longest journeys of my life. I could feel the quivering of the unfortunate bird as it was quietly bleeding to death in my grasp. My mother quickly finished her off. I suppose we ate that turkey, although I cannot remember that part. Mam had no qualms whatsoever about killing fowl, regardless of whether it was goose, duck, turkey or chicken. She would often require me to assist her in this task, holding the unfortunate bird by the legs as she cut its throat. I could feel the violent reaction of the victim in my hands. It was a job I really hated. I was most definitely not cut out for farm life.

Joe's old Ferguson tractor ran on petrol, not diesel, thus the engine had ignition components to deliver electrical pulses to the spark plugs. Part of our experience of growing up was to stand beside the stationary tractor whilst the engine was running and while Joe was not looking, then reach out and touch some of the exposed electrical parts, just to see if you could take the shock, and, more to the point, to see if you had the courage to do it in the first place. It wasn't as bad as it sounds, but it took guts all the same. Another similar trial was to grasp and hold on to an electric fence. These were deployed to contain cattle within particular areas. An electric shock ran through the fence every second or so. If your timing was good, you could grasp the wire just between pulses, thus avoiding the shock altogether. But that was regarded as somewhat unmanly. The real test was to grasp and hold on for several seconds. Like the experiment with the tractor, the fear and the anticipation involved was much worse than the actuality. Of course the ultimate test of manliness was to urinate on such a fence, but I was never tempted to try that.

Another example of the laid-back nature of Joe O'Connor's temperament occurred one Sunday morning as Dad was driving us all to Mass. Joe was in the car in front, and he pulled up to give somebody a lift. Either Dad was not watching the road carefully enough, or, more likely, the brakes were practically non-existent, as usual. In any case, he drove into the rear of Joe's car. Rather than leap from his vehicle to inspect the damage and heap invective on the head of the guilty party whilst shouting "Whiplash!" Joe simply remained where he was, behind the wheel. He sat there and barely turned his head, as Dad reported on the situation, which was not very serious. And that was the end of it.

Other agricultural contractors were hired from time to time, particularly for harvesting cereal crops in the autumn. This meant the arrival of the combine harvester, by far the most impressive machine we would see in the course of a year. In later years I would get to climb on board and help out with the operation, but as a small boy I was only allowed to stand and watch, awestruck at the power of the entire operation. A local pair of brothers, John and 'Junior' Taaffe were among the contractors who went from farm to farm with a combine harvester. The machines were not the most reliable, regularly breaking down, and needing a degree of attention. I vividly recall such an occasion when they were working in one of our fields. One of the brothers, I think it was John, actually climbed right into the bowels of the machine in order to clear whatever obstruction was causing the problem. We lost sight of him completely, until suddenly he pushed out a hinged flap halfway down the side of the harvester and waved out to us. I was shocked to see him entombed like that, and was scared that the machine might start up by accident. The even more horrific possibility was that Junior might not realise where John had got to and might casually go and start the thing up, thus rendering his own brother into little grain-sized pieces.

Some of the neighbouring farmers would become exceedingly anxious and nervous about the arrival of agricultural contractors to take care of harvesting their cereal crops. They genuinely found it difficult to assist in a useful manner, without doing more harm than good. When our nearest neighbours observed that I was able to cope (probably just about) with the flow of grain aboard the combine harvester, they requested me to perform the same function while the machine was in their fields. I was happy to do so, and so that became another annual fixture in my calendar, until I left home.

Mrs Hayes

The nearest shop, about a mile away from our place, was owned and run by Mrs. Hayes. Located in the family home, the shop was really tiny, not much more than the size of a large bathroom. The Hayes family also ran a small farm, in which most of the work seemed to be performed by Mrs Hayes herself. Her husband, Stephen, appeared to be disabled; certainly he rarely stirred out from the kitchen. You would hear his voice call out from inside;

"How's the ould lad?" meaning my Dad. "Would he still know you?" For years he seemed to think such derogatory remarks were really funny. Mrs Hayes, by contrast, was nearly always jolly and generous. Once you arrived at the shop, the first task was to locate her, or wait for her, as she was almost always engaged in farmyard activities, such as milking cows, feeding pigs, looking after hens and so on. When she finally was ready behind the counter, her next remark would be;

"Have you a ticket?"

A "ticket" meant a list of groceries, usually written out by my mother. As she checked each item, she would remark;

"You'll have to git it".

There was no cash register or any other modern convenience in the shop, so she would tot up the total cost on the same scrap of paper, the so-called "'ticket', using the remaining stub of a pencil, probably no more than an inch in length. Finally, she would always offer a sweet from a jar, with the remark;

"Here, you can be chewin' goin' over the road."

Mrs Hayes was not licensed to sell alcohol, the cost of such a license being prohibitive, I suppose. However, she did actually keep bottles of Guinness for sale, carefully concealed from open view. When called upon to do so, she could make these bottles appear, as if by magic. A few bottles of Guinness, or 'stout', or indeed 'porter' as it was called, were always kept in every farmhouse for the specific purpose of being given to visiting agricultural contractors, along with their dinner. Nowadays, all such contractors bring their own food with them and the very idea of consuming alcohol whilst operating agricultural machinery is something that died out with the 1970's. When stout was required from Mrs Hayes, a codeword had to be used. I loved the very idea of a codeword. My mother's written list would simply contain the special word 'messages', accompanied by the quantity. This way there was no written record of any illegal activity.

The shop was licensed to sell tobacco products however. Indeed, smoking was generally so prevalent that a shop that did not sell cigarettes and pipe tobacco might as well not have opened its doors at all. A small painted sign in the glass panel above the front door announced to the world that Mrs Hayes' shop was licensed for this purpose. Apparently, the words had been painted there by our Dad, many years before. I always glanced up at the sign, taking a little pride in it. Outside the shop, there was a flat metal advertising sign on the wall, extolling the virtues of a type of pipe tobacco called 'Garryowen Plug". Alongside a picture of what looked like an Irish Setter dog, the slogan was intended to read "Smoke Garryowen Plug. It satisfies." The significance of the dog escapes me. The way the slogan was printed on the sign, it actually read "Smoke Garryowen. It satisfies Plug." To us, Plug was one of the characters in the Bash Street Kids. I used to wonder how smoking a type of tobacco named after a place in Limerick could possibly satisfy the needs of a cartoon character in the Beano. Those old signs were outside every shop that sold tobacco. Now, you will only find them in modern Irish pubs that are pretending to be a hundred years old, in an effort to pull the wool over the eyes of gullible tourists.

Some of the products in the shop were still measured out in the old-fashioned way. Sugar, for example, and raisins also, were weighed on a scale, balanced against a series of weights, until the desired amount was reached. I loved watching the process as Mrs Hayes adjusted the thing until it just about balanced. I imagine that weighing systems like that can only be seen in a museum now. I loved raisins (I still do) and, eventually, I somehow stumbled upon the realisation that a half pound of raisins was much better value than a half pound of sweets. At last - I could afford to buy my own stuff! Mrs Hayes was smart enough to understand that my mother was not making fruit cakes every week. She was also smart enough not to turn down trade, no matter whether it held parental approval or not. And so now, an escalation of activities was called for. A box of matches – now, there was something that held a particular fascination for a small boy. What could be better than starting your own fire in the heart of the countryside? We would, of course, regularly purchase matches for genuine reasons; after all they were needed for lighting the fire in the range, for operating the gas cooker, and also for Dad, who was a smoker. Mrs Hayes, though, had a pretty shrewd idea of just how many boxes of matches a family was likely to need over any given period of time, so when I first began to cheat a little and actually buy matches just for myself, she smelled trouble.

"Is that box of matches for your father now? Or are they for yourself, by any chance?" she would ask.

"They're for my father", I lied. She had no option really, other than to take my word for it. Oh, the exultation that comes from having your own box of matches in your pocket! Perhaps that is how an arsonist feels, I don't know. Anyway, I never actually did any damage with the matches, but I suppose I could have.

It's slightly ridiculous now when one considers the things that one coveted as a small child; and it was not just raisins and matches. I absolutely loved the taste of golden syrup, for example, and my dream of adulthood was to be able to afford a tin of the stuff all to myself. It came in a green tin, and was manufactured by Tate and Lyle - I believe it still is. There was something fascinating, whilst also slightly disgusting about the picture on the cover of a swarm of bees hovering above what looked like the body of a dead lion, accompanied by the rather peculiar slogan, "Out of the strong came forth sweetness." I never understood that and I still do not. Surely bees produce only honey, and certainly not golden syrup, which I understand to be a by-product of sugar manufacturing. And what kind of bees would hang around a dead lion anyway? We had our own honey, and I knew perfectly well, as would any aficionado of all things sweet, that the flavour of golden syrup is quite a distinct and different thing to that of honey. In any case, I imagined how marvellous it would be to greedily scoff the entire contents of the tin in one sitting. Now, of course, we have the stuff sitting for months at a time on a shelf in a kitchen cupboard. I also remember seeing advertisements for Cadbury's 'Crunchy' bars in a magazine, and knowing, even though I had not yet tasted one, that it would be wonderful. The same applied to ads for 'Bounty' bars – the slogan in this case being, 'The Taste of Paradise'. These magazine ads were just plain black and white drawings, not even photographs; simple to the point of being quite primitive by today's sophisticated standards. But they worked extremely well for me. Of course, such exotic fare was not available in the local country shops, and so I tasted these products in my imagination, long before I came upon them for real. And, in fairness, they did not disappoint.

From a child's point of view, the one major disadvantage of Mrs Hayes shop was that she did not have a fridge or freezer, thus there was no ice-cream to be had. Luxury of that nature necessitated a longer journey of more than two miles in the opposite direction to Mrs. Ryans' shop in Tubber village. My mother regularly supplied eggs to Mrs. Ryan. These were to be subsequently sold in the shop, or at least I assumed so. Transporting eggs in a shopping bag that swung from the handlebars of my bicycle sometimes meant breakages, but this was not regarded as a major issue, rather being seen as a kind of inevitability, a casualty of the logistics in use, one might say. As soon as the necessary financial transactions had been got out of the way, the really interesting business could then begin i.e. which ice-cream to select. When you were assigned the job of going to the shop, the implicit understanding always was that you could spend some of the change you got back on whatever delicacy you chose. If the change was just a few 'coppers' i.e. one or two pence, then one's options were limited to an ice-pop; very basic stuff. However, if 'silver' such as sixpence was available, a whole new vista of opportunities opened up, like a choc-ice, for example, or a 'Brunch', or possibly a slice of ice-cream cut off the block and served between wafers. Of course, no system is perfect and the disadvantage of Mrs. Ryans' shop was that she never gave out any sweets for free as Mrs. Hayes did.

Ryans' shop also stocked lollipops - for two pence each, I think. When I say pence, I actually mean the pence part of pounds, shillings and pence. On Saturday evenings, about once a month or so, we were taken to attend Confession in the chapel just across the road from Ryans' shop. The confession part was a total ordeal, but afterwards we always got lollipops at the shop. The special thing about these lollipops was that each one contained what we called a 'transfer'. This was a miniature picture that you peeled apart and then stuck on your arm, giving the appearance of a very crude tattoo. I don't really know why we prized them as highly as we did, since they were usually worn away by the time we got home. The lollipop almost lasted as long.

Printed in Great Britain
by Amazon

46972321R00116